Good Cooking
Sylvia P. Gerson

L'Chaim + Bon Appétit
Mildred L. Covert

KOSHER SOUTHERN-STYLE COOKBOOK

KOSHER SOUTHERN-STYLE COOKBOOK

By Mildred L. Covert
and Sylvia P. Gerson

Illustrated by
ALAN GERSON

Foreword by
RABBI GAVRIEL NEWMAN

PELICAN PUBLISHING COMPANY
GRETNA 1993

The word "Pelican" and the depiction of a pelican are
trademarks of Pelican Publishing Company, Inc., and are
registered in the U.S. Patent and Trademark Office.

Library of Congress Cataloging-in-Publication Data

Covert, Mildred L.
    Kosher southern-style cookbook / by Mildred L. Covert and
Sylvia P. Gerson ; illustrated by Alan Gerson ; foreword by Gavriel
    Newman.   p.   cm.
    Includes indexes.
    ISBN 0-88289-850-7
    1. Cookery, American—Southern style.   2. Cookery, Jewish.
I. Gerson, Sylvia P.   II. Title.
TX715.2.S68C685   1992
641.5′676′0975—dc20   92-15413
                                          CIP

Manufactured in the United States of America

Published by Pelican Publishing Company, Inc.
1101 Monroe Street, Gretna, Louisiana 70053

To our children and grandchildren
who inspire us to continue
our creative cooking.

Contents

Foreword

My dear friends Mildred and Sylvia have "cooked up" another wonderful book for you. This one is even saucier than its predecessors. Arranged in an original format, it takes you on a tasteful tour of the South, providing fascinating points of historic and scenic interest for all the southern states.

Not enough attention has been paid to the historic grand Jewish community of the South, which plays a central role in American Jewish history. Perhaps this cookbook addresses this problem by putting us in touch with the unique, distinct flavor of southern-style cooking according to Jewish custom. Nobody could tell the story of the Jewish South more elegantly than these two southern belles, Mildred and Sylvia. Dynamic, intelligent, effervescent, spicy, and beautiful; they are everything our community could wish for. You will enjoy reading their words almost as much as you would meeting with them in person.

I delight in seeing the care and attention that the authors have given to our sacred tradition and dietary custom. The recipes are carefully constructed to conscientiously guarantee that the traditional and non-traditional alike can prepare these dishes, without infracting biblical or rabbinical law. A small word of caution to the traditional minded: When recipes call for nondairy creamer or margarine, be sure to check for the "pareve" definition on the product label. The Food and Drug Administration did not have pareve in mind when they defined nondairy. Also, Worcestershire sauces are now made with fish content, which precludes its use with meat, by custom. Check the label and ingredients before using with meat.

This cookbook is proof of the contention, now becoming more of a proven fact in America, that keeping Kosher does not mean restricting the appeal and taste of the dishes we eat. So eat and enjoy!

RABBI GAVRIEL NEWMAN
Beth Israel Congregation
7000 Canal Boulevard
New Orleans, Louisiana 70124

Introduction

Is it true what they say about Dixie?
Does the sun really shine all the time?
Do the sweet magnolias blossom
Round everybody's door?
Do the folks keep eatin' possum
'Till they can't eat no mo'?

The South is on the rise again—not with cannons booming nor sabers flying, but with their best weapon: *food*. No matter what southern state you are in, eventually the focus turns to food. All agree (that is, all southerners) that of all the regional cooking traditions, southern is by far the tastiest.

As each southern state was settled, cooks brought their recipes from home. However, they learned quickly that grits, fried chicken, and corn fritters could replace kasha, Yorkshire pudding, wiener schnitzel, and various other foods from home. Each southern state had a special and distinct flavor of its own. This is the charm of the South. The Confederacy has a story of its own.

Over 100 years ago, eleven southern states seceded from the Union, forming the Confederacy. Each of these states had something special to offer the South, be it their geography, their life-style, or their industry. There was one thing they all had in common—southern hospitality. Food played an important role in this tradition. Generation after generation, southerners have continued to demonstrate this hospitality, and where better to extend a warm and loving welcome than from the kitchen?

The southern women, like our Jewish grandmothers, spent much of their time in the kitchen preparing food with love and care for their families and guests. They each had their own style, but they both measured by the feel of the ingredient rather than cups or spoons.

They would scoop up a handful of flour or sugar, feel the weight, and invariably, it was just exactly right. Few recipes were written down prior to the 1860s. Measurements, as we know them today, were unheard of. When it came to measuring, they would scoop up butter the size of an egg or walnut; liquids were measured in egg shells; and the recipe always came out just right. They used "a pinch of this" or "a pinch of that" to add extra flavor to the pot. The foods that came from the kitchens of the Confederacy were as hearty and delicious as any presented today.

Southern Jewish women adapted their households to the southern way of life. They helped manage plantations; they lost their European accents to the Southern drawl; and more importantly, they brought into their kitchens the rich culinary heritage of the area in which they lived. Throughout the generations, one thing remained constant—the foods from their kitchens remained Kosher.

In this, our third book, by way of introduction, we have prefaced each chapter with an authentic original Civil War or pre-Civil War recipe. We hope that you will be able to follow, with ease, the transition of other southern recipes that we have re-created. We believe y'all will come away from the table sated and singing the melody, "That's what I like about the South."

MILDRED L. COVERT
and
SYLVIA P. GERSON

KOSHER SOUTHERN-STYLE COOKBOOK

SOUTH CAROLINA
The Palmetto State

South Carolina: beauty, charm, culture, and history. It is nicknamed the Palmetto State, not only because of the abundance of palmetto trees along the coast, but also because the ramparts of Fort Moultrie, the site of the defeat of the British fleet in 1776, were built of palmetto logs. In 1777, the year following the British defeat, South Carolina adopted the palmetto as its flag emblem and official state seal.

The original colony was founded by the English but colonized by the French Huguenots (Protestants seeking religious freedom). In the years following its establishment as a colony, it became a haven for French Huguenots, English, Scotch-Irish, Welsh, and Germans—all seeking religious and economic freedom. Together, they created the state of South Carolina.

The coastal areas of the state proved to be ideally suited for the growing of rice, indigo, tobacco, and sugar. Before long, plantations were cropping up all along the coastline. The newcomers developed townships inland. Their backgrounds were entirely different from the early settlers, the landed aristocracy, thereby adding another dimension to the cultural character of South Carolina.

In the antebellum days the state began to flourish; economic conditions were favorable and slavery, the topic of the day, was also becoming a political issue. By the early 1800s, the move toward secession was gaining momentum. Tempers were rising as swiftly as the tariffs. Finally, in 1860 in Charleston, the Ordinance of Secession was passed, making South Carolina the first state to secede from the Union. The first shot was fired at Fort Sumter in Charleston Harbor on April 12, 1861; soon thereafter, the federal garrison fell to the Confederates and remained in their hands until the evacuation of Charleston in 1865.

Post-war South Carolina suffered during its occupation by federal troops. The carpetbaggers from the North raided the treasury, leaving the state heavily in debt. It would be decades before South Carolina would emerge from the devastation she suffered during and after the Civil War. Soldiers returning home were faced with salvaging their homes and their land. With the loss of property came the creation of a new way of life. Before long, new plantations began to appear upon the horizon. However, the wise fathers knew that South

Carolina could no longer be just an agrarian state, so they looked for a new industry.

The textile industry slowly began to take hold and South Carolina found a new approach to financial success. South Carolina began to stabilize economically when the wise fathers became aware of the state's natural resources, its climate, and its 300 years of history. Diversification became the byword of the 20th century, and tourism was born.

Today, South Carolina is a popular vacation spot. All year long, visitors enjoy the recreational facilities at the seashore, mountain resorts, and, of course, the historic sites. In Charleston, you will find K.K. Beth Elohim, the oldest synagogue in continuous use in the United States since its dedication in 1794. Santee Cooper Country, Columbia, and Lexington offer attractions that continue to draw tourists to the Palmetto State.

As a visitor, you will be lured by the smells and tastes of South Carolina's very special food. There are real down-home grits, red-eye gravy, and hash. Additionally, there is "Gullah" cooking, made popular by the Gullah-speaking Afro-American descendants of slaves. The Gullahs consider themselves to be the Atlantic Creoles.

As you travel along the Atlantic Coast, stop and feast on golden fried or broiled seafood. You will find your plate heaped with piles of coleslaw and those crispy balls of fried cornmeal known as hush puppies. In the Charleston area, where fine dining has become a form of art, the menus feature seafood soups, Huguenot torte, and chocolate mud pies.

When you leave, you will take with you a wide variety of historical and culinary experiences. Come see South Carolina because "nothing could be finer than to be in Carolina."

COUNTRY SYLLABUB

Mix half a pound of white sugar with a pint of fine cider or white wine, and grate in a nutmeg. Prepare them in a large bowl, just before milking time. Then let it be taken to the cow, and have about three pints milked into it, stirring it occasionally with a spoon. Let it be eaten before the froth subsides. If you use cider, a little brandy will improve it.

REBEL COCKTAIL

5 cups vegetable juice
2 cups water
2 tsp. Kosher
  instant beef soup mix

¼ cup Worcestershire sauce
¼ cup Scotch
2 tbsp. lemon juice
6 lemon wedges

Heat vegetable juice, water, soup mix, and Worcestershire sauce in a large saucepan to boiling; then simmer until soup mix is dissolved. Stir in Scotch and lemon juice. Serve hot in mugs garnished with lemon wedges. Serves 6.

COLONEL CALHOUN'S CANAPE

2 cups flaked smoked trout
2 cups finely chopped
  celery
2 hard-cooked eggs,
  finely chopped

1 tsp. black pepper
1 tbsp. grated onion
  and juice
¾ cup mayonnaise

Mix all ingredients together until well blended. Mound on small rounds of white or rye bread or crackers. Makes about 4 dozen canapés.

COLONIAL SLAW

⅓ cup salad oil
1 tbsp. sugar
2 tbsp. lemon juice
2 tbsp. prepared
  yellow mustard

½ tsp. salt
2 carrots, sliced
4 cups shredded cabbage
1 green pepper, chopped

Combine oil, sugar, lemon juice, mustard and salt in bowl or covered jar. Stir or shake until well blended. Pour over vegetables and toss to mix. Serves 6.

PALMETTO HUSH PUPPIES

2 cups yellow cornmeal
1 tbsp. sugar
2 tsp. baking powder
1 tsp. salt
½ tsp. baking soda

1 egg, beaten
2 tbsp. vegetable oil
1 cup buttermilk
1 large onion, finely chopped
vegetable oil for deep frying

Combine the dry ingredients in a mixing bowl. Combine the egg and 2 tablespoons of vegetable oil; then add them to the dry ingredients along with enough of the milk to make a very thick batter. Add the chopped onion and stir just until dry ingredients are moistened.

Drop batter by tablespoon into hot oil (375°). Fry for about 2 minutes until golden brown, turning once. Makes about 2 dozen.

BEAU'S BARBECUED FISH

1 3- to 4-lb. fish
½ tsp. salt
dash pepper
1 tbsp. vegetable
   shortening
2 tbsp. chopped onions

2 tbsp. vinegar
2 tbsp. brown sugar
3 tbsp. Worcestershire
   sauce
1 cup tomato catsup
⅓ cup lemon juice

Place the fish in a greased shallow pan, and sprinkle with salt and pepper. Lightly brown onions in vegetable shortening; then add the remaining ingredients. Simmer 5 minutes; then pour over the fish. Bake in a 425° oven for 35 to 40 minutes. Baste fish with sauce while cooking. Serves 6.

FRAYLACH FISH STEW

2 10¾-oz. cans
   condensed tomato soup
1 14-oz. bottle tomato
   catsup
½ lb. onions, sliced
   thin
½ stick butter
¼ tsp. Worcestershire sauce

1 tsp. pepper
dash cayenne pepper
1 tbsp. salt
1 cup water (optional)
6 medium freshwater fish,
   deboned, skinned, and
   cut into small pieces

Combine soup and catsup and slowly bring to a boil. Sauté the onions in the butter until tender, then add them and the other ingredients, except the fish, to the soup mixture. If too thick, add the water. Boil 5 minutes. Drop in the fish pieces and cook about 5 more minutes. Serve over rice or with hush puppies. Serves 6.

BIG DADDY'S POT ROAST

1 4- to 5-lb. pot roast
2 to 3 tbsp. vegetable
  oil
1 cup chopped onions
1 cup chopped celery

1 cup chopped carrots
1 cup chicken broth
1 cup Kosher cooking wine
water

Cook the roast in oil in a dutch oven over medium heat until brown; then remove it from the dutch oven and add the vegetables. Cook until the vegetables brown. Return the roast to the dutch oven and add the broth, wine, and enough water to cover the roast. Cover and simmer for 2 to 3 hours, until tender, turning the roast once. Remove roast to a warm platter and serve with gravy. Serves 8.

TUNKLER TURKEY HASH

1 large red potato
2 tbsp. pareve
  margarine
½ cup minced onions
1 clove garlic, minced

¼ cup minced red, yellow,
  and green pepper
2 cups minced leftover turkey
⅓ cup leftover gravy
salt and pepper to taste

Peel and dice the potato. Put it into a pan and cover with lightly salted water. Bring to a boil; then reduce the heat and simmer for 12 to 15 minutes until cooked. Drain.

Melt pareve margarine and sauté the onion, garlic, and bell peppers over moderate heat for 5 minutes. Add the potatoes, turkey, and gravy. Heat thoroughly and season to taste. Serves 4.

CAROLINA CHICKEN

2 tbsp. olive oil
1 fryer chicken (about
 2 lb.), quartered
1 bunch shallots, chopped
1 8-oz. can sliced mushrooms

½ tsp. crushed red
 pepper
1 bunch parsley, stems
 removed and chopped
2 cups chicken broth

In an iron skillet or other heavy pot, heat the olive oil over medium heat. Pat chicken pieces dry, then brown them on all sides in the hot oil. Remove the chicken and set it aside.

In the same skillet, sauté shallots, mushrooms, and crushed red pepper until the white portions of the shallots turn glossy. Return the chicken to the pot; add the parsley and the broth. Reduce the heat and cover with a lid or aluminum foil. Simmer for 45 minutes, stirring occasionally to prevent sticking. Serves 4.

CO-CHER CHICKEN STEW

2 chicken breast halves,
 skin removed
1½ cups water
¼ tsp. salt
2 whole cloves
1 bay leaf
⅔ cup frozen mixed
 vegetables
⅔ cup potatoes, pared
 and diced

½ cup chopped onion
¼ cup sliced celery
1 cup chopped ripe tomato
¼ tsp. ground thyme
⅛ tsp. pepper
¼ cup flour
¼ cup water

Cover chicken with the water, add the salt, cloves, and bay leaf; and cook about 45 minutes or until tender. Remove the chicken from the broth, and separate the meat from the bones. Dice the chicken.

Skim the fat from the broth, remove the cloves and bay leaf, and add enough water to the broth to make 2 cups. Cook the mixed vegetables, potatoes, onion, and celery in the broth for 10 minutes.

Add the chopped tomato, thyme, and pepper to the broth mixture. Cook for 15 minutes; then add the chicken pieces.

Mix the flour into the water until smooth. Stir it into the chicken mixture; and cook, stirring constantly, until thickened (about 1 minute). Serves 4.

DIXIE CHICKEN

1 large cut-up fryer	1 tsp. chopped parsley
salt and pepper	1/8 tsp. paprika
1 cup flour	3/4 cup nondairy creamer
1/3 cup pareve margarine	1/4 cup water
1 tbsp. chopped celery	

Preheat the over to 375°. Season chicken pieces with salt and pepper; then dredge them in flour. Melt the margarine in a baking dish or casserole. When smoking hot, place the chicken in the casserole, and place it in the oven. Let the chicken brown lightly, then add the celery, parsley, and paprika.

Combine nondairy creamer with the water. Mix well. Pour the liquid over chicken. Cover the dish tightly, then bake in the hot oven until tender, about 1½ hours.

When the chicken is tender, remove the cover and continue to bake for about ½ hour, or until chicken is nicely brown on top. Serves 4 to 5.

BROTHER'S BEETS

(Microwave)

1 lb. beets (about
10 2-inch beets)
½ cup water
2 shallots with tops
1 lemon
2 tbsp. butter or
margarine

1 tsp. balsamic or red wine
vinegar
1 tsp. dijon mustard
½ tsp. salt
¼ tsp. pepper
1 tbsp. chopped fresh
parsley

Cut the leaves off of the beets, leaving one inch of stem. Wash the beets well. Put the beets and water in a round, microwavable baking dish and cover it with plastic wrap. Microwave on high power for about 15 minutes, until tender when pierced with a fork. Stir three times while cooking. When done, let stand, uncovered, for 3 minutes; then drain. Peel and cut into thin slices when cool enough to handle.

Put butter or margarine in a microwavable baking dish. Microwave, uncovered, on high until melted, about 1 minute. Slice the shallots and grate ⅛ teaspoon zest from the lemon. Stir shallots into the melted butter and microwave, covered and vented, on high for about 3 minutes until soft. Stir in the vinegar, mustard, lemon zest, salt, and the sliced beets. Microwave, covered and vented, on high for about 2 minutes until heated through. Stir in the pepper and sprinkle with parsley. Serves 4.

CALLEY'S CREAMY CORN

(Microwave)

1 17-oz. can cream-
style corn
1 cup half-and-half or milk
½ cup sliced shallots
or green onions

3 tbsp. butter or margarine
3 eggs, lightly beaten
salt and pepper to taste

Combine the corn, milk, shallots (or green onions), and butter in a 4-cup glass bowl. Microwave at high power for 5 to 6 minutes, stirring once, until mixture is hot and bubbly.

Beat eggs lightly in a 5- to 6-cup microwave casserole. Gradually blend the hot corn mixture into the eggs, stirring rapidly to prevent lumping. Season to taste with salt and pepper.

Cover the casserole with wax paper. Microwave at 50 percent power for 5 to 7 minutes, or until custard is almost set in the middle. Stir once after 3 minutes. Let it stand, covered, on a heatproof surface until serving time. Serves 4.

HAMISH HOPPING JOHN

1 cup dried field peas	4 slices Beef Frye, fried
4 cups water	(reserve grease)
2 tsp. salt	1 medium onion, chopped
1 cup uncooked rice	

Boil the peas in salted water until tender. Combine the peas and 1 cup of the pea liquid with the rice, Beef Frye, reserved grease, and onion. Put the mixture in a rice steamer or double boiler and cook for 1 hour until rice is thoroughly done. Serves 8.

SUMTER'S SUCCOTASH

½ cup sieva beans	½ cup raw corn, cut from
(or butter beans)	cob
1½ cups water	2 tbsp. butter
1 tsp. salt	salt and pepper to taste

Boil sieva beans in the salted water until tender, but not soft. Add the raw corn and cook until tender. Drain, add butter, and season to taste. Serves 4.

HOPPIN' YANKEL
(Microwave)

6 slices Beef Frye, diced
1 medium onion, chopped
1 bay leaf
8 oz. dried black-eyed
  peas, soaked and ready
  to cook

1 cup rice
3 cups hot tap water
fresh parsley or sliced
  green onion tops
  (optional)

Combine Beef Frye, onion, bay leaf, drained black-eyed peas, and rice in a 4-quart casserole. Pour the hot water over the ingredients in the casserole; cover. Microwave on high for 10 minutes; then microwave on 30 percent (medium-low) for another 30 minutes.

Let stand for 10 to 15 minutes for liquid to be absorbed. Remove the bay leaf before serving, and garnish with parsley or green onion tops. Serves 8.

MAMMY'S MASHED POTATOES

1½ lb. potatoes,
  with skins
¼ cup milk

3 tbsp. butter
1 tsp. salt
½ tsp. pepper

Cut potatoes into chunks. Put them in a pot with enough salted water to cover them. Bring to a boil, covered; then cook, uncovered, for about 25 minutes until tender. Drain, peel, and mash the potatoes. Combine the milk and butter in a saucepan and heat until warm. Stir the mixture into the mashed potatoes along with the salt and pepper. Serves 4.

RUNAWAY RED RICE

3 slices Beef Frye, diced
1 cup chopped onions
1 cup chopped tomatoes
1 cup uncooked rice
½ tsp. salt

¼ tsp. ground black pepper
pinch cayenne pepper
1¾ cups water
2 tbsp. tomato paste
1 tbsp. water

Cook Beef Frye in a small skillet over low heat until almost crisp; then remove it from skillet and set aside.

Pour Beef Frye drippings into medium-sized saucepan; then cook the onions in the drippings until golden. Stir in the tomatoes, rice, salt, black pepper, cayenne pepper, and 1¾ cups of the water. Bring the mixture to a boil, stirring once or twice. Reduce the heat, cover, and simmer for 15 to 20 minutes until rice is tender and the liquid is absorbed. Blend the tomato paste with the tablespoon of water. Stir tomato paste and reserved Beef Frye into the rice. Serves 6.

CHUTZPA CUSTARD

1 qt. milk
5 eggs, separated

5 tbsp. sugar
1 tsp. vanilla extract

Heat the milk in a small saucepan. Cream egg yolks and sugar thoroughly; then add the warm milk slowly. Beat the egg whites until foamy (but not too stiff), and fold them into the mixture. Add the vanilla; then pour into a casserole dish, or individual custard dishes. Set the dish in a pan of hot water; then place in a 325° oven and bake for about 1 hour, or until an inserted knife comes out clean. Serves 6.

HUGUENOT TORTE

4 eggs
3 cups sugar
8 tbsp. flour
5 tsp. baking powder
½ tsp. salt

2 cups peeled, chopped, tart
   cooking apples
2 cups chopped pecans or
walnuts
2 tsp. vanilla extract

Beat the eggs with an electric mixer or rotary beater until very frothy and lemon-colored. Add the remaining ingredients in order. Pour the mixture into two well-buttered 8x12-inch baking pans. Bake in a 325° oven for about 45 minutes until crusty and brown. To serve, scoop up with a spatula, keeping crusty part on top, and pile on a large plate or individual plates. Cover with whipped cream and a sprinkling of chopped nuts. Serves sixteen.

MOONSHINE WHISKEY CAKE

½ cup butter
1 cup sugar
3 eggs, beaten
1¾ cup flour
½ tsp. baking powder
¼ tsp. salt
½ tsp. nutmeg

¼ cup milk
¼ tsp. baking soda
¼ cup molasses
1 lb. seedless raisins
2 cups chopped pecans or
walnuts
¼ cup bourbon

Cream the butter and sugar together in a bowl; then stir in the eggs. Combine the flour, baking powder, salt, and nutmeg; then stir the flour mixture into the butter mixture. Stir in the milk. Mix the baking soda with the molasses, and stir into the butter mixture. Stir in the raisins, nuts, and bourbon; then pour the mixture into two 8½x 4½-inch greased and floured loaf pans. Bake at 300° for 2 hours. Allow them to cool before removing from pans. Wrap in foil and store in refrigerator. Makes two loaves.

MISSISSIPPI
The Magnolia State

A land of sunshine and rain, productive soil, and mild climate, Mississippi is one of the world's great cotton-growing regions. The state is named for the Mississippi River (known as the Father of Waters) which flows along the state's western boundary. The name, Mississippi, came from two Indian words meaning "great river" or "great waters." The state's nickname, the Magnolia State, is appropriately chosen for the flowering magnolia trees growing throughout the state.

Eight flags have flown over Mississippi—an indication of its rich historic and romantic past. Hernando de Soto, a Spaniard, was the first white man to enter the present state of Mississippi. It is believed that he and his adventurers came to the area searching for gold as early as 1540. Instead, they discovered the mighty Mississippi River. Robert Cavelier Sieur de LaSalle later claimed the land for France; and Natchez was established in 1716 as an outpost of the French coastal colony.

The Treaty of Paris brought the land under British rule, but their reign came to an early end when the Spanish returned to Mississippi to set up their colonial government in Natchez. When the region became a territory of the United States in 1798, Natchez was designated its capital and remained the capital when Mississippi was admitted to the Union as the 20th state. It was not until 1821 that Jackson was named the new capital in honor of General Andrew Jackson. It remains the capital city today.

The new state of Mississippi boomed throughout the first half of the 19th century. Fortunes were made from the fertile land and the river. Cotton was king! A great, wealthy cotton empire grew, bringing in new people and commerce. During these years, cotton-based fortunes provided many plantations with the means to a gracious lifestyle. When the slavery issue began dividing the nation, Mississippi sided with the southern states. Dreams and fortunes of many people collapsed when, in January of 1861, Mississippi adopted the Ordinance of Secession, making it the second state to secede from the Union.

The Civil War left Mississippi economically devastated. In the days of the Reconstruction, the state limped along. The dishonest and extravagant carpetbaggers and scalawags drained the state of its wealth. It took more than twenty-five years for Mississippi to recover from losses sustained during and directly after the Civil War.

After 1875, the economy of the state depended heavily on cotton and timber. In Piney Woods, the tung oil industry was started in the early 20th century, and farming remained, as always, important to the state. However, the economy has changed greatly since the Great Depression of the thirties. Many new manufacturing plants have been constructed. Since World War II, industrial and agricultural activities have continued to increase throughout the state.

Perhaps nowhere else in the country do the history and beauty of the South come together as in the state of Mississippi. There is so much to see and do in the Magnolia state. The scenery is gorgeous in the hills, and the stunning sunsets of the Delta region linger long in your memory. The plains are full of legends, adventure, and excitement—Indian land of mystery and beauty. The historic battlegrounds of Vicksburg, the grace and enchantment of Natchez, and the distant whistles of the riverboats, are the proud reminders that you are in the beautiful heartland of Mississippi. The sound of waves breaking gently on the beach, a soft ocean breeze, and mouth-watering seafood are just a few of the pleasures of the Mississippi Gulf Coast.

No matter what part of the state you are in, you will notice the warmth and cordiality extended by Mississippians. Along with their unique historical heritage, they offer you an equally unique regional cuisine. Mississippi is home cooking to haute cuisine.

Come see—come taste—Mississippi. You will leave singing its praises to the tune of "M-I-S S-I-S S-I-P-P-I!"

BEEF AND BEANS

Take a piece of brisket of beef, cover it with water, when boiling skim off the fat, add one quartern of French beans cut small, two onions cut in quarters, season with pepper and salt, and when nearly done take a dessert-spoonful of flour, one of coarse brown sugar, and a large teacup full of vinegar, mix them together and stir in with the beans, and continue stewing for about half an hour longer.

YANKEE GO HOME COCKTAIL

4 egg yolks
nutmeg to taste
4 tsp. sugar

1 qt. rich milk
4 jiggers whiskey

Beat yolks, sugar, and seasoning together. Add milk and whiskey. Shake well with crushed ice, strain, and serve. Serves 8 to 10.

WHEEZIE'S WATERMELON RINDS

2 cups watermelon rind
  cubes
⅓ cup cornmeal
⅓ cup all-purpose flour

1 tsp. salt
¼ tsp. freshly ground black
  pepper
1 cup vegetable shortening

With a knife, peel the rinds by cutting off the dark outside skin and inner layer down to the white part. Cut the white part of the rind into half-inch cubes.

Mix together the cornmeal, flour, salt, and pepper. Heat the shortening to 350° in a heavy, 10-inch iron skillet. Roll the cubed rinds in the cornmeal mixture; then add them to the hot oil. Fry for about 8 to 10 minutes until lightly browned. Stir gently; then cook for about 4 to 5 minutes more until browned all over. Drain on paper towels and season with salt and pepper. Serve hot. Makes 2 cups.

CHEESE WAFERS FROM CHELM

1 lb. sharp cheddar
  cheese, grated
¾ cup margarine

2 cups all-purpose flour
1 cup toasted pecans,
  chopped
½ tsp. cayenne pepper

Let cheese and margarine stand at room temperature until soft; then mix them together in a large bowl until smooth. Add the rest of the ingredients and mix until well blended. Form into rolls about 1 inch in diameter. Wrap in waxed paper and chill or freeze until firm. Slice into ⅛-inch wafers. Place on an ungreased cookie sheet and bake at 400° for 10 to 12 minutes until lightly browned. Cool on a wire rack. Makes about 6 dozen.

ODILEE OKRA SOUP

1 large beef bone with
  plenty of meat
3 qt. water
3 lb. fresh okra,
  chopped fine
1 Kosher smoked sausage,
  sliced in ½-inch
  pieces

8 large fresh tomatoes, peeled
  (or 2 28-oz. cans tomatoes)
1 bay leaf
2 medium onions, chopped
salt and pepper to taste

In a soup pot, cook meat bone in water slowly over low heat for two hours. Add the okra, smoked sausage, peeled tomatoes, bay leaf, and onions. Salt and pepper to taste. Cook another 2 hours, adding more water if needed. Serves 8 to 10.

DANDI-LION SOUP

1 lb. dandelion greens,
chopped
1 lb. Kosher smoked sausage,
cut into 1-inch pieces
1 large onion, chopped
1 tsp. vinegar

8 cups water
2 cups raw potato, peeled
and cubed
1 16-oz. can black-eyed
peas, including liquid
salt and pepper to taste

In a soup kettle, combine the greens, sausage pieces, onion, vinegar, water, and potato. Bring the soup to a boil, then lower the heat and simmer for about 1½ hours. Add black-eyed peas and their liquid. Salt and pepper to taste. Serves 6 to 8.

FISH FROM THE OVEN

1½ lb. fish fillets,
skinned and cut into
4 pieces
⅔ cup finely chopped
pecans
⅔ cup grated parmesan
cheese

2 tbsp. butter
1 tbsp. vegetable oil
salt and pepper to taste
lemon wedges

Preheat the oven to 450°. Rinse the fish under cold water and pat very dry. Combine pecans and parmesan cheese thoroughly and pour them onto flat casserole plate.

Dip each fish portion in the butter-oil mixture. Season with salt and pepper; then dip into pecan-parmesan mixture until mixture adheres.

Place fish portions on a cookie sheet. Bake for about 10 minutes per inch thickness of fish. Serve with lemon wedges. Serves 4.

FRESSER'S FRITTERS

1 whole fish (about 1 to
   1½ lb.)
3 eggs, separated
3 tbsp. flour
½ tsp. salt

⅛ tsp. pepper
⅛ tsp. minced garlic
1 tbsp. minced parsley
vegetable oil for deep frying

Boil the fish until the meat is flaky and white. Remove the skin and bones and mash the meat. Beat egg yolks until light and thick; then add the flour, salt, pepper, garlic, parsley, and mashed fish. Beat the egg whites until stiff and fold them in the fish mixture. Drop by tablespoons into hot oil (360° to 370°), and fry until brown. Serves 4.

ROYTA SNAPPER
(Microwave)

1 small tomato, peeled,
   seeded, and chopped
½ cup chopped onion
½ cup chopped green
   pepper
¼ cup margarine
1 4-oz. can sliced and
   drained mushrooms
3 tbsp. chili sauce

2 tbsp. lemon juice
2 tbsp. capers
1 tbsp. snipped parsley
1 clove garlic, minced
½ tsp. dried thyme
¼ tsp. salt
1 tsp. hot pepper sauce
2 lbs. red snapper fillets
¼ cup dry white wine

Combine all the ingredients, except the fish and wine, in a 12x7x 2-inch glass baking dish. Cover with waxed paper, and microwave at 100% power for 5 to 6 minutes until vegetables are tender. Stir in the wine. Place fish fillets on top and spoon some of the sauce over the fish. Cover and cook for 4 to 5 minutes at 100% power, or until the fish flakes when pierced with a fork. Serves 6.

SCALAWAG CHICKEN STRIPS

½ cup all-purpose flour
½ tsp. salt
½ tsp. paprika
¼ tsp. pepper
¼ tsp. thyme
¼ tsp. onion powder

¼ tsp. garlic powder
⅛ tsp. crumbled sage
1½ lb. skinless boneless
   chicken breast halves
½ cup vegetable oil

In a paper bag, combine the flour, salt, paprika, pepper, thyme, onion powder, garlic powder and sage. Shake to combine. Cut the chicken into 2½ by ¾-inch strips; then place the chicken strips in the bag and shake until well coated.

In a large skillet, heat ¼ cup of the oil until hot but not smoking. Working in batches, add a single layer of chicken to the skillet, leaving about ½ inch between each piece. Sauté over moderately high heat until crisp and golden brown, about 3 minutes. Transfer the chicken to a platter lined with paper towels to drain; then sauté the remaining chicken, adding more oil if necessary. Serve hot. Serves 4.

PASCAGOULA POULET

1 3-lb. chicken
½ cup flour
1 tsp. salt
¼ tsp. pepper
4 tbsp. vegetable shortening

2 cups chicken stock
1 16-oz. can petit pois green
   peas, drained
1 2-oz. jar chopped pimentos

Cut chicken into serving pieces of legs, thighs, wings, and breasts. Combine the flour, salt, and pepper. Rub each piece of chicken thoroughly with the seasoned flour.

Melt the vegetable shortening in an iron skillet on low heat. Drop in the chicken, and brown on both sides. Add the chicken stock, stir to prevent sticking; then cover and simmer for 1 to 1½ hours. Add the green peas and pimentos during the last 20 minutes. Serves 4.

MAGNOLIA MEAT LOAF MIT SAUCE

2 lb. ground beef
1 cup cornbread crumbs
1 large onion, chopped

1 large bell pepper, chopped
2 eggs, beaten
½ 8-oz. can tomato sauce

Mix all the ingredients together and form them into a loaf. Place in baking pan or a 9x5x3-inch loaf pan. Prepare the sauce and pour it over the meat loaf. Bake for 1 hour and 10 minutes at 350°. Baste several times while baking. Serves 8.

Sauce

1 cup water
2 tbsp vinegar

2 tbsp. dark molasses
2 tbsp. prepared mustard

Combine all the ingredients, mix thoroughly, and pour over meat loaf. Makes 1 cup.

REVIVAL VEAL RIBS

3 to 4 lb. veal ribs
1 tsp. salt
¼ tsp. pepper
2 onions, sliced
2 tsp. vinegar
2 tsp. Worcestershire
sauce

1 tsp. salt
1 tsp. paprika
½ tsp. red pepper
½ tsp. black pepper
1 tsp. chili powder
¾ cup catsup
¾ cup water

Select meaty veal ribs. Cut into servings or leave whole. Sprinkle with the 1 teaspoon of salt and the ¼ teaspoon of pepper. Place in a roaster pan and cover with the onions. Combine the remaining ingredients, then pour the mixture over the meat. Cover and bake at 350° for about 1½ hours. Baste occasionally and turn the ribs once or twice. Remove the cover for the last 15 minutes to brown the ribs. Serves 6.

HOPPIN' JOHN BOY

2 cups water
1 tbsp. unsalted
  butter or pareve
  margarine
1 tsp. salt

½ tsp. Tabasco sauce
1 cup converted rice
1 16-oz. can black-eyed peas,
  drained
¼ tsp. black pepper

In a large saucepan, bring the 2 cups of water to a boil. Stir in the butter (or pareve margarine), salt, Tabasco sauce, and rice. Return to a boil; then reduce the heat to low, cover and simmer for about 20 minutes until the rice is tender.

Add the black-eyed peas and pepper to the rice. Simmer over very low heat, stirring occasionally, for about 5 minutes until the beans are warmed through. Serves 4.

TUPELO TURNIP PUFFS
(Conventional and Microwave)

2 lb. turnips, pared
  and cubed
2 medium cooking apples,
  pared, cored, and sliced
boiling water
2 cups dry bread crumbs

½ cup butter or margarine,
  melted
2 tbsp. sugar
4 eggs, beaten
2 tsp. salt
¼ tsp. pepper

CONVENTIONAL: Place the turnips and apples in enough boiling water to cover them. Cook for 20 to 30 minutes until very tender. Drain and mash the turnip mixture, leaving it lumpy. Mix in the remaining ingredients; then spoon into a greased 1½-quart casserole. Bake at 375° for 1 hour or until golden. Serves 6 to 8.

MICROWAVE: Combine the turnips, apples, and ¼ cup water in a 3-quart glass casserole; cover with plastic wrap and microwave at high power for 15 to 20 minutes until very tender. Drain and mash; then mix in the remaining ingredients. Spoon the mixture into a greased 1½-quart glass casserole. Cover with plastic wrap and microwave at high power for 10 to 12 minutes or until set. Rotate the dish ¼ turn every 4 minutes. Let stand, covered, for 5 minutes before serving. Serves 6 to 8.

MISS LOU'S FRIED GRITS

3½ cups water	1 large egg
¾ cup white hominy grits	¼ cup all-purpose flour
½ tsp. salt	2 tbsp. salad oil
½ lb. sliced Beef Frye	maple syrup

In a 3-quart saucepan over high heat, bring the 3½ cups of water to boiling. Slowly stir the grits and salt into the boiling water and bring back to boiling. Reduce the heat to low, cover, and simmer for 25 to 30 minutes, stirring occasionally, until all liquid is absorbed.

Pour the grits into a greased 8½x4½-inch loaf pan. With a metal spatula, smooth the top; then cover and refrigerate for about 4 hours (or overnight) until the grits are cold and firm.

About 45 minutes before serving, cook the Beef Frye in a 12-inch skillet over medium-low heat until browned and crisp. Remove the Beef Frye and drain on paper towels. Keep warm. Discard the drippings and wipe the skillet clean.

Invert the chilled grits from the loaf pan onto a cutting board. Cut into ½-inch-thick slices. In a shallow dish, beat the egg slightly. Place the flour on waxed paper. Dip the grits slices, one at a time, in the beaten egg, then in the flour to coat lightly. In the same skillet over medium-high heat, heat the salad oil. When salad oil is hot, fry the grits slices until golden brown on both sides. Serve the fried grits with Beef Frye slices and maple syrup. Serves 4.

DUVID'S DELTA RICE

1 cup long grain rice
4 tbsp. melted pareve
　margarine
2½ cups boiling chicken
　broth
1 medium onion, chopped
1 green pepper, chopped
1 clove garlic, chopped

2 stalks celery with leaves,
　chopped
3 sprigs parsley, chopped
2 tbsp. cooked button
　mushrooms
½ cup slivered almonds
¼ tsp. powdered oregano

Sauté the rice in the pareve margarine until golden. Pour the rice into a 2-quart casserole; then add the broth. Cover and bake at 350° for 30 minutes. Cook the onion, green pepper, garlic, celery, and parsley in the remaining pareve margarine until soft and clear. Stir them into the rice, add the remaining ingredients, and bake for 30 more minutes. Serves 6.

OLDE SOUTHERN KOSHER KORNBREAD

1¾ cups yellow cornmeal
¼ cup flour
1 tsp. salt
1 tsp. baking powder
1¼ cups buttermilk

½ tsp. baking soda
2 eggs
2 tbsp. melted butter
　or margarine

Combine the cornmeal, flour, salt, and baking powder; mix well. Combine the buttermilk and baking soda in a small bowl; then beat until foamy. Add the buttermilk mixture to cornmeal mixture. Beat in the eggs; then stir in the melted butter or margarine. Pour into a greased hot skillet. Bake in a 450° oven for 20 minutes or until lightly browned on top. Serves 8.

HOT SOURMASH SUNDAES

½ cup chopped pecans
1 tbsp. plus 1 tsp.
  unsalted butter
½ cup honey
1 tbsp. dark brown sugar

¼ cup water
2½ tbsp. sourmash, bourbon,
  or rye whiskey
1 pint vanilla ice cream

In a small skillet over moderate heat, sauté ¼ cup of the pecans in 1 tablespoon of the butter until the nuts are lightly browned, about 2 minutes.

In a small saucepan, combine the honey, brown sugar, and water. Bring to a boil over high heat and continue to boil for 2 minutes. Remove from the heat and add the remaining 1 teaspoon of butter. Stir until melted; then stir in the whiskey.

Place a generous scoop of ice cream in each of 4 chilled dessert dishes. Top each portion with 1 to 2 tablespoons of the hot whiskey sauce and sprinkle with the remaining chopped pecans. Serves 4.

MISSISSIPPI MUD PIE

1 9-inch pie pastry
¼ lb. butter (1 stick)
3 1-oz. squares un-
  sweetened chocolate
3 eggs

3 tbsp. light corn syrup
1½ cups sugar
1 tsp. pure vanilla extract
vanilla ice cream (optional)

Preheat the oven to 350 degrees. Line a 9-inch pie plate with the pastry.

Combine the butter and chocolate in a saucepan. Heat gently, stirring often, until both are melted and blended together. Beat the eggs until light and frothy. Stir the corn syrup, sugar, and vanilla into the eggs; then pour in the melted chocolate mixture, stirring.

Pour the filling into the prepared pie plate. Bake 30 to 40 minutes, or until the top is slightly crunchy and the filling is set. Do not overcook. The filling should remain soft inside.

Either serve warm with a spoonful of vanilla ice cream on top, or at room temperature or cold. Serves six to eight.

MISSISSIPPI MUD CAKE

½ lb. butter
2 cups sugar
4 eggs
1½ cups flour
⅓ cup cocoa

1 cup coarsely chopped
    pecans
1 tsp. vanilla extract
3 cups kosher marshmallows,
    cut into ½-inch pieces

Preheat the oven to 350°. Combine the butter and sugar in a mixing bowl, and beat until creamy. Add the eggs, one at a time, beating thoroughly after each addition.

Sift together the flour and cocoa; then fold it into the creamed mixture. Add the cup of chopped nuts and the vanilla, and beat well.

Butter the bottom and sides of a 9x13-inch baking pan. Add a little flour and shake it around to coat the bottom and sides of the pan; then shake out the excess flour.

Spoon the cake mixture into the pan and smooth it over. Place in the oven and bake at 350° for 30 to 35 minutes. Remove from the oven and sprinkle the top with marshmallows. Return to the oven and bake for about 10 minutes until marshmallows are melted and starting to brown. Remove from the oven and let cool in the pan for about 30 minutes. Serves 12 or more.

Icing

½ lb. butter
1 lb. confectioners' sugar
⅓ cup cocoa

1 cup coarsely chopped
    pecans
½ cup evaporated milk

Melt the butter in a saucepan. Sift together the confectioners' sugar and cocoa. Stir the sugar mixture into the butter along with the nuts and milk. Spread the icing over the cake and let stand until thoroughly cold. Ices one 9x13-inch cake.

FLORIDA
The Sunshine State

Florida, a semitropical state, a land of flowers and sunshine, is referred to as the Sunshine State, the Peninsula State, and the Everglade State. Today, it is a haven for tourists and a mecca for people who relish the warmth year-round. Florida is one of the fastest growing states in the nation.

On Easter Sunday, more than 400 years ago, Ponce de Leon, who was lured to the New World by the promise of gold and the Fountain of Youth, spotted the Florida Coast and claimed it for Spain. He named it Florida because of the profusion of vivid flowers. (The Spanish word *florida* means "flowering".) Ponce de Leon explored Florida from coast to coast, and he found a land of beaches, golden sand, mineral springs (perhaps they do have rejuvenating powers), spectacular climate, and exciting geography—more precious and lasting than he ever imagined.

From this beginning came the nation's oldest settlement, St. Augustine, as well as the nation's gateway to the stars—the Kennedy Space Center.

Florida is a very special place. After many unsuccessful attempts to cultivate and settle this wilderness by trying to develop plantations like the rest of the Deep South, settlers came to the realization that Florida was different. In the rest of the South, farmers were able to easily adjust their lifestyles from the Old World to their New World farms of familiar crops. This was not the case in Florida. The people, not the land, would have to change.

As the Carolinas and Georgia became increasingly crowded and plantation land became scarce, more and more English colonists began to move toward Florida. The Spanish only colonized the beachheads of Florida and never realized the true richness of the state. Therefore, in 1763, Spain decided to cede Florida to England. Oddly enough, however, the first wave of settlers were not Englishmen, but Greeks, Italians, and Minorcans. They raised indigo and found their food in the sea. Soon, indigo gave way to small citrus farms. The Minorcans found that adapting themselves to the land was much easier than trying to force the junglelike land to adapt to them.

However, in 1845, when Florida was admitted to the Union, little settlement was taking place. Great cotton plantations worked by slaves were established in the northern part of the state, while sugar plantations dominated the southern part. The slave-holding plantation system produced nearly all of the wealth in the state. It was not surprising that Florida sided with the South in the Civil War. On January 10, 1861, Florida became the third state to secede from the Union.

Although Federal troops easily occupied the coastal towns, Tallahassee, the capital city then and now, was the only Confederate state capital that was not captured. Throughout the war, control of Jacksonville and Duval county bounced back and forth between northern and southern forces. Fortifications (some still remain) were built by one side or the other, only to be captured or abandoned.

Amelia Island Plantation, resting just off Florida's northernmost Atlantic coast, was once the home of French, Spanish, and English colonists. Pirates, we are told, once raided the Spanish Main from a base on the island. Fort Clinch, a massive brick Civil War structure, was strategically located to watch enemy fleets put out to sea. The fort now stands in a designated state park.

The Reconstruction ended the plantation system in Florida. Out of the turmoil came a rediscovery of Florida. Spending the winter in Florida had long been recommended for the infirm; and after the Civil War, the Sunshine State became a popular winter resort. It became fashionable to spend the winter in the sun's warmth. Pleasure became a serious pastime. Promising the perfect vacation, tailored to your taste, the Sunshine State beckoned one and all. Florida has kept this promise.

As you enter northwestern Florida, the Emerald Coast greets you with the legendary Seminole Indian territory. From there, you can go to see astronauts, in central eastern Florida, known as the Space Coast. Across the state is the Gulf Coast with beautiful sunsets, vistas of the Gulf of Mexico, and big city life. The southwestern coast is yet to be discovered for the most part. Smack in the center of the state is Disney World, and finally, there is the Gold Coast of southeastern Florida, flaunting its sunshine all year long.

Yes, Florida is indeed a very special place. Whatever your pleasure, Florida offers a potpourri of the best in recreation: fun on the beaches, fact-filled historical attractions, fantasy in Disney World, and food from all over the world. Gourmands vacillate from Cuban to

Creole delicacies: tropical mangoes, key lime pies, fritters, seafood chowder, and paella. No matter what your destination is in Florida, you'll enjoy it all, from "way down upon the Suwannee River" to the "Moon Over Miami."

POTATO SHAVINGS

Take four fine large potatoes, and having peeled them, continue to cut them up as if peeling them in ribbons of equal width; then throw the shavings into a frying-pan, and fry of a fine brown; they must be constantly moved with a silver fork to keep the pieces separate. They should be laid on a cloth to drain, and placed in the dish lightly.

GALITZIANER GOYSTERS

1 egg
½ cup water
½ cup white cornmeal
¼ tsp. pepper (or to taste)

3 gefilte fish pieces
(about 2½ inches long)
vegetable oil for deep frying

Make an egg wash by beating the egg and water together. Combine the cornmeal and pepper; then spread it on a platter or flat surface. Slice the gefilte fish into twelve ½-inch-thick slices. Dip the gefilte fish slices into the egg wash; then roll them in the seasoned cornmeal. Chill for ½ hour.

Deep fry in vegetable oil at 350° for 3 to 4 minutes. Cook a little longer for extra crispness. Serve with either lemon juice, ketchup, hot pepper sauce, or horseradish. Serves 2.

SADIE'S SPREAD

¼ cup shredded green
  pepper
¼ cup peeled and shredded
  cucumbers
¼ cup shredded radishes

¼ cup shredded shallots,
  scallions, or green onions
2½ 8-oz. pkg. cream
  cheese, softened

Place the shredded vegetables and cream cheese in a food processor bowl fitted with a metal blade. Pulse on and off until all ingredients are mixed well. Chill and serve with bagel chips. Makes 3 to 4 cups.

CANAPES FROM THE CAPE

1 7½ oz. can red salmon
1 tbsp. minced onion
1 12-oz. pkg. cream
  cheese
1 tbsp. fresh chopped dill

12 rye toast rounds or
  crackers
chopped dill pickle or
  fresh parsley

Drain the liquid from the salmon; then mash the salmon with a fork. Add the minced onion, cream cheese, and chopped dill and mix well. Spread on toast rounds or crackers. Garnish with chopped dill pickle or chopped parsley. Makes 1 dozen canapés.

ORLANDO SALAD

1½ cups diced oranges
1½ cups shredded raw
  carrots
½ cup seedless raisins
1 tsp. grated orange rind

Tangy French Dressing
  or Honey French Dressing
  (see recipes)
lettuce leaves

Combine oranges, carrots, raisins, and orange rind. Moisten with desired dressing and serve on lettuce leaves. Serves 5 to 6.

MICKEY'S DRESSING

1 tsp. salt
⅛ tsp. cayenne pepper
¼ tsp. black pepper
½ tsp. dry mustard
1 tsp. Worcestershire
  sauce

1 tbsp. finely minced
  onion
1 clove garlic, finely minced
2 tbsp. white vinegar
6 tbsp. salad oil

Combine all ingredients in a bowl; then beat with a rotary or electric mixer until well blended. Chill. Shake before serving. Makes about ½ cup dressing.

MINNIE'S DRESSING

2 tbsp. honey
½ tsp. salt
¼ tsp. paprika

3 tbsp. lemon juice
6 tbsp. salad oil

Combine honey, salt, paprika, and lemon juice; then mix well. Gradually beat in the oil. Makes ¾ cup dressing.

SPACE SHUTTLE SALAD

3 medium-sized tomatoes, peeled and sliced
1 onion, peeled and cut into rings
Assorted salad greens
⅓ cup Lift Off Salad Dressing (see recipe)

¾ tsp. celery seed
¼ cup pickle relish
6 slices Beef Frye, cooked and crumbled
3 hard-cooked eggs, quartered

Arrange tomato slices alternately with onion rings on salad greens. Combine salad dressing, celery seed, and pickle relish; then pour it over the tomatoes and onions. Sprinkle Beef Frye crumbs on top. Garnish with egg sections. Serves 6.

LIFT OFF DRESSING

2 tsp. salt
1 tsp. sugar
½ tsp. pepper
1 tsp. paprika

½ cup vinegar (cider, malt, tarragon, or wine vinegar)
1½ cups salad oil or olive oil

Combine all ingredients in a covered jar and shake well. Chill. Shake again before using. Makes 2 cups.

SUWANNEE RIVER KATZFISH CHOWDER

20 lb. large whole
  fresh fish, scaled
  and gutted
20 lb. potatoes,
  peeled and cubed
4 1-lb. cans tomatoes
2 8-oz. cans tomato
  sauce
10 lb. onions, chopped

1 lb. butter or
  margarine
10 bay leaves, crumbled
2 tbsp. thyme
1 bag Crab Boil
  seasonings
½ cup Worcestershire
  sauce
salt and pepper to taste

Place the fish in a large pot, cover it with water, and bring it to a boil. Reduce the heat to simmer until fish is well done. Drain the fish and pour the liquid back into the kettle. Remove fish meat from the bones and place the meat in the kettle. Add the potatoes and remaining ingredients and simmer for 2 hours, stirring frequently. Serve with crackers or hot French bread. Makes 40 servings.

FLORIDIAN FILLETS

2 lb. fresh fish
  fillets
3 tbsp. butter or
  margarine, melted
2 tbsp. fresh orange
  juice

2 tsp. grated orange
  zest
1 tsp. salt
dash allspice
dash pepper

Preheat the oven to 350°. Cut the fillets into 6 portions. Place the fish in a single layer, skin side down, in a well-greased 12x8x2-inch baking dish.

Combine the remaining ingredients; then pour the sauce over the fish. Bake for 15 to 20 minutes until fish flakes easily when tested with a fork. Garnish with orange twists if desired. Serves 6.

SARATOGA STUFFED SNAPPER

1 3- to 4-lb. red snapper,
  scaled and gutted
1 tsp. salt
¾ cup chopped celery
½ cup chopped onion
¼ cup vegetable oil
4 cups dry bread cubes

½ cup sour cream
¼ cup diced lemon
2 tbsp. paprika
1 tsp. salt
2 tbsp. butter
  or margarine, melted

Sprinkle the snapper inside and out with 1 teaspoon of the salt. Cook the celery and onion in vegetable oil until tender. Add the bread cubes, sour cream, lemon, paprika and 1 teaspoon of salt. Mix thoroughly; then stuff the snapper and secure the opening with small skewers or toothpicks. Place in a well-greased baking pan and brush with the melted butter or margarine. Bake in 350° oven for 45 to 60 minutes until fish flakes easily when tested with a fork. Brush occasionally with the butter or margarine. Remove skewers before serving. Serves 3 to 4.

SHTETL FRIED CHICKEN

1 2½- to 3-lb. frying
  chicken, cut up
1 medium onion, chopped
4 tbsp. pareve margarine
1 bell pepper, chopped
1 cup rice

2 tomatoes, chopped
2½ cups water
salt to taste

Brown the chicken pieces and onions in pareve margarine. Place in a casserole dish. Mix the remaining ingredients together and pour them over the chicken. Cover. Bake at 350° for 40 minutes until the chicken is tender and the rice is done. Serves 4.

KLEZMER CHICKEN

1 stewing chicken, cleaned
and innards removed
1 8-oz. pkg. flat egg
noodles
1 16-oz. can tomato sauce
1 8-oz. can tomato paste

2 onions, chopped
1 green pepper, chopped
½ cup peeled and chopped
celery
2 tsp. oregano
salt and pepper to taste

Place the stewing chicken in a large pot. Cover it with water and simmer for about 50 to 60 minutes until it is tender. Remove the chicken from the broth and set it aside to cool on a plate.

Cook the noodles in the remaining broth according to package directions until they are almost tender. Add the remaining ingredients, cover, and simmer until the vegetables are tender.

While the vegetables are cooking, remove the chicken from the bones. Add the chicken meat to the pot just before the vegetables are done. Serves 6.

TEVYE'S TONGUE

1 3-lb. tongue
1 large onion, chopped
1 stalk celery, chopped
1 green pepper, chopped
1 cup raw mushrooms

3 tbsp. schmaltz or
vegetable shortening
1 16-oz. can green peas,
drained
1 10½-oz. can tomato soup

Boil the tongue about 1½ hours or until it is tender. Allow it to cool; then peel, slice and put it in a 2-quart casserole dish.

In a large skillet, sauté the onion, celery, green pepper, and mushrooms in smaltz or vegetable shortening. When the vegetables are tender, add the peas and tomato soup. Pour the mixture over the sliced tongue. Bake in the oven at 350° for 1 hour. Serves 6.

MY-AMI'S MEATLOAF
(Conventional and Microwave)

2 lb. lean ground beef
1 cup fresh bread crumbs
½ cup minced onion
½ cup nondairy creamer
¼ cup ketchup
2 eggs, well beaten
2 tsp. salt

¼ tsp. freshly ground
pepper
1 tsp. oregano
1 tomato, sliced
1 tsp. browning sauce (for
microwave method only)

MICROWAVE: Combine the meat, bread crumbs, onion, nondairy creamer, ketchup, eggs, salt, pepper, and oregano. Mix well. Spoon into a 12x8-inch glass baking dish. Shape into an 8x5-inch loaf, making the ends square rather than oval. Mix browning sauce with one teaspoon of water; then brush it over the meat. Arrange a row of tomato slices along the top of the loaf. Cover tightly with plastic wrap, turning back an edge to vent. Microwave at 70% power for 28 to 30 minutes. Let stand 5 minutes; then lift it out of the baking dish and place it on a warm platter. Serves 6 to 8.

CONVENTIONAL: Preheat the oven to 350°. Combine the meat, bread crumbs, onion, nondairy creamer, ketchup, eggs, salt, pepper, and oregano. Mix well. Spoon into 12x8-inch baking pan and shape into 8x5-inch loaf. Arrange a row of tomato slices along the top of the loaf. Bake for 1 hour and 15 minutes. Let stand 5 minutes before serving. Serves 6 to 8.

A VINTER VEAL STEW

1 lb. boned veal shoulder
3 cups cold water
2 tsp. monosodium
  glutamate
2 lb. fresh green beans
3 tbsp. pareve
  margarine
3 tbsp. flour

1 tbsp. sugar
1 tsp. salt
⅛ tsp. pepper
2 tbsp. vinegar
¼ tsp. summer savory
1 tbsp. chopped parsley

Cut the veal into ½-inch pieces. Place the veal pieces in a pot with the cold water and 1 teaspoon of the monosodium glutamate. Bring slowly to boil; then lower the heat and simmer for 1 hour. Wash the beans, break off the tips, and remove any strings. Break the beans into 1-inch pieces, add to veal, and cover. Cook for 25 minutes until tender.

Melt the pareve margarine; then blend in the flour, sugar, salt, and remaining monosodium glutamate.

Remove the liquid from green bean mixture; then add enough water to it to make it total 4 cups. Add the water and the vinegar to the flour mixture. Cook, stirring, until smooth and thickened; then add it to the green bean mixture. Mix in the savory, parsley, and pepper. Cook, uncovered, over low heat for 15 minutes. Serves 6.

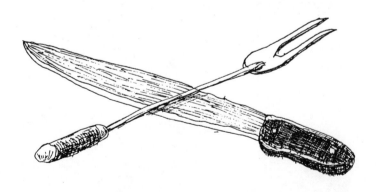

RICE & SPICE & EVERYTHING NICE

½ cup chopped celery
½ cup chopped onions
1 tbsp. butter or
    margarine
1 tsp. salt
⅛ tsp. ground
    allspice
⅛ tsp. ground
    cinnamon

⅛ tsp. ground black pepper
1 tbsp. brown sugar
3 cups cooked rice
½ cup raisins, plumped
1 tart cooking apple, cored,
    peeled, and chopped
½ cup sliced almonds,
    toasted

In a large skillet, cook the celery and onions in the butter or margarine until tender and crisp. Add the seasonings, rice, and raisins. Heat thoroughly. Stir in the apple; then remove from the heat. Cover and let stand 5 minutes. Sprinkle with almonds. Serves 6.

EVERGLADE EGGPLANT

1 large eggplant
¾ tsp. salt
juice of 1 small onion

1 large egg (or 2 small eggs)
1 cup bread crumbs
1 tbsp. butter or margarine

Peel the eggplant; then cut it into quarters. Place the quartered eggplants in enough water to cover them, and boil until fairly tender. Drain and mash the pulp. Add the salt, onion juice, egg, and enough bread crumbs to create the consistency of pudding. Place the mixture in a greased 1½-quart casserole. Sprinkle the top with additional bread crumbs and dots of butter or margarine. Bake at 350° for about ½ hour, or until brown. Serves 4.

PINCUS POLE BEANS

1 lb. pole beans
¼ lb. pastrami, cubed

1 medium onion, sliced
in thin rings

Rinse the beans, remove the tips, and cut them into 1-inch pieces. Place the beans in pot with enough water to cover them. Add the cubed pastrami, cover, and cook over a medium fire for 20 minutes until the beans are crisp and tender. Garnish with onion rings. Serves 6.

ZEESE POTATO PONE

2½ cups grated sweet
   potatoes
1 cup sugar
2 eggs, beaten
1 tbsp. grated orange
   rind

1 tsp. nutmeg
2 tbsp. butter, melted
1 cup chopped nuts
¼ tsp. cinnamon
¾ cup milk

Combine all ingredients, mix well, and place in a greased casserole. Dot the top with additional butter. Bake at 350° for about 45 minutes, or until golden brown. Serves 6.

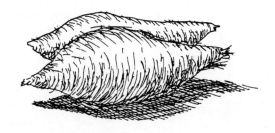

FENCY-SHMENCY FRUIT PIE

1 16-oz. can seedless
   sour cherries, drained
1 20-oz. can crushed
   pineapple, drained
2 cups sugar
6 tbsp. cornstarch
¼ tsp. red food coloring

dash salt
6 sliced bananas
1 cup chopped nuts
2 9-inch graham cracker
   crumb crusts
1 pint whipped cream

In 2-quart pot, place the drained cherries and pineapple. Add the sugar, cornstarch, food coloring, and salt. Cook over medium heat until thick, stirring occasionally. Add bananas and nuts; then pour into 2 graham cracker crusts. Top with whipped cream. Keep refrigerated. Makes two 9-inch pies.

B'NANNY PUDDIN'

2 cups milk
2 eggs, beaten
⅔ cup sugar
⅛ tsp. salt
2 tbsp. cornstarch

1 tsp. vanilla extract
48 vanilla wafers
   (28-oz. box)
4 bananas, diced

Combine the milk, eggs, sugar, salt, and cornstarch in the top of a double boiler and beat with an electric mixer until smooth. Place over hot water and cover. Cook, stirring occasionally, until thick; then cool. Stir in the vanilla. Place alternate layers of vanilla wafers, diced bananas, and custard in a 1½-quart casserole. Cover and chill before serving. Serves six.

PONCE DE LEON'S LIME PIE

6 eggs
2 cups sugar
juice of 5 to 6 limes
  (about ⅔ cup juice)
¼ cup butter, melted

1 9-inch graham cracker
  pie crust
whipped cream
lime slices

Preheat the oven to 325°. In a mixing bowl, beat the eggs lightly. Add the sugar, lime juice, and butter; then beat until blended. Pour the mixture into the prepared pie crust. Bake for 30 to 35 minutes, or until the filling is set and the crust is golden. Cool; then refrigerate for several hours. Just before serving, top with whipped cream and garnish with lime slices. Serves eight to ten.

ALABAMA
The Cotton State

In the heart of the Deep South lies the state of Alabama, named for a tribe of Indians of the Creek Confederacy called the *Alibamu,* "thicket clearers" or "plant gatherers." Cotton was once the chief crop of Alabama's plantations; thus, the state became known as the Cotton State. Another popular nickname is the Yellowhammer State. During the Civil War, a company of Alabama soldiers paraded in fancy uniforms, trimmed in brilliant yellow—reminiscent of the gaily colored birds called flickers or yellowhammers. Incidentally, the yellowhammer was adopted as the state bird.

Alabama is a interesting blend of the old and the new—a combination of unspoiled natural splendor and every comfort of modern times. Long before the white man settled Alabama, thriving tribes of Cherokee, Creek, Choctaw, and Chickasaw Indians populated this large tract of land. These were the inhabitants that would greet Hernando De Soto in 1540—the first white man to arrive in Alabama. Staking a Spanish flag in the soil, De Soto claimed the territory for Spain.

The Spanish did little to colonize their newly claimed territory. It was almost 200 years before any real settlement took place. When early French explorers found themselves trekking through a strip of land near what is now Mobile Bay, they dubbed it Dauphin Island, in honor of Louis XIV's oldest son, the Dauphin of France. The French built a fort on the island and began colonization in earnest. The first permanent colony was Mobile, founded on its present site by the French in 1711.

The territory was bandied back and forth during the mid-1700s, alternating between Spain, France, and Great Britain. Finally, in 1783, Alabama was ceded to the United States.

Great changes swept through Alabama in the years to follow. Two settlements in Alabama, known then as East Alabama and New Philadelphia, were prospering from brisk river commerce. News of their success began to spread, and pioneers began to settle faster than ever. The two cities, once rivals, decided to merge in 1819 to form Montgomery, named in honor of Revolutionary War hero General Richard Montgomery. In 1846, Montgomery was chosen to be the state capital.

King Cotton ruled over the acres of farmland. Plantation owners lived in opulence—nothing surpassed the grandeur of Alabama's antebellum social life. Slavery made it possible for a continuance of economic growth. It was no wonder, and certainly no surprise, that Alabama considered itself a paragon of Confederate policies. On January 11, 1861, Alabama became the fourth state to secede from the Union. It was at the Alabama Secession Convention that the Confederacy was brought into official existence. Montgomery, often referred to as the "Cradle of the Confederacy," was selected as its first capital. On the steps of the State Capitol in 1861, Jefferson Davis took the oath of office as President of the Confederacy.

Once again, Alabama was subjected to a great deal of change. Alabama became a strategic battlefield during the war. The "Rebel yell" could be heard from the state's northernmost boundaries to the Gulf Shores. It was during the Battle of Mobile Bay that Union Admiral David Farragut is credited with shouting, "Damn the torpedoes, full speed ahead." Interestingly, Mobile was the only major Confederate port to avoid Union occupation.

After the Civil War, Alabama fell into hard times. The glittering antebellum social life became a thing of the past. Plantations deteriorated due to forced neglect. The Reconstruction took its toll on the Cotton State where, ironically, cotton was no longer king. Undaunted, Alabamians believed that the South would rise again; and, through perseverance and determination, indeed it would.

Industrial cities like Birmingham began to emerge. Steel mills were being built, industry was diversifying, and Birmingham became the manufacturing center of the South.

Prosperity continued unabated until the Great Depression. Once again, Alabama's economy sprang back. The need for materials during the second World War had the Gulf ports bustling and the industrial centers producing as never before. Where cotton crops once predominated, there were now vegetables, fruits, nuts, livestock, and poultry. Birmingham, instead of concentrating on industry alone, erected what was to become one of the outstanding medical centers of the nation; thus presenting Alabama with a new image.

As the 21st century approaches, Alabama has emerged as a state with special charms. The influences of many cultures have made it a fascinating state to live in or visit. Its regional culture and cookery strongly reflect the many changes that the state has undergone. The colonists and their ensuing generations enriched and altered their lifestyles—and styles of cooking—as they adapted to the American way of life. The result is a mixture of the best of all worlds.

Alabama beckons one and all to come, explore, and enjoy. As a visitor, you will be welcomed warmly and invited to return often. Pack your bags and, when asked where you're headed, sing out: "I'm Alabamie Bound."

SAUERKRAUT

To make sauerkraut, place a 2 to 3-inch layer of thinly shredded cabbage into a large stone or earthen crock. Sprinkle lightly with salt. Pound vigorously with a potato masher or wooden "stomper." Repeat this process until crock is almost full. Cover with a clean cloth and place round board on top. Place something on top of board to weigh it down heavily. Set in warm place to ferment. In about 6 days, remove the scum that has formed on top. Wash the cloth in cold water, replace it and move the crock to a cool place. In about two weeks the sauerkraut will be ready.

JEZEBEL JULIP

2 tsp. orange peel
2 tsp. lime peel
½ cup orange juice
½ cup lime juice
2 tbsp. sugar

2 tbsp. chopped fresh mint
4 cups melon balls (watermelon, honey dew, and cantaloupe)
1 cup lemon-lime carbonated beverage, chilled

Combine the peels, juices, mint, and sugar. Pour over the melon balls. Chill for at least two hours. Just before serving pour the carbonated beverage over fruit. Serves 4.

TUSCALOOSA TUNA BALL

1 8-oz. pkg. cream cheese, softened
1 6½-oz. can solid white tuna, drained and flaked
3 tbsp. diced green pepper
3 tbsp. diced onion
3 tbsp. diced celery
5 pimiento-stuffed olives, diced
2 tsp. prepared horseradish
½ tsp. Tabasco sauce
½ tsp. Worcestershire sauce
½ cup chopped pecans

Combine all the ingredients, except the pecans. Stir well. Shape into a ball. Cover and chill for at least one hour. Roll the ball in the chopped pecans. Cover and chill. Serve with assorted crackers. Makes about 2 cups.

ALABAMA BISCUITS

1 pkg. yeast
4 tsp. sugar
2½ cups flour
1 tsp. salt
2 tsp. baking powder
4 tbsp. vegetable shortening
¾ cup milk
¼ cup butter

Dissolve the yeast and 1 teaspoon of the sugar in a small amount of warm water. Combine the dry ingredients and the remaining sugar in a mixing bowl; then cut in the shortening. Stir in the milk and yeast mixture; then roll out to about ½-inch thick on lightly floured board. Cut with a biscuit cutter, dip each biscuit into the melted butter, and place on a baking sheet. Cover and let rise for 1 hour. Bake at 450 degrees for 10 to 12 minutes. Makes about 12 to 15 biscuits.

FARRAGUT'S FRIED BREAD

1 cake dry yeast
1½ cups lukewarm milk
2 eggs
4 cups flour
1 tbsp. sugar

2 tsp. salt
oil for deep frying
additional salt to taste
1 large clove garlic, split

Dissolve the yeast in the warm milk in a mixing bowl. Add the eggs and mix well. Sift together the flour, sugar, and the 2 teaspoons of salt. Stir the flour mixture into the yeast mixture. Add slightly more flour if necessary to make the dough manageable but still very sticky. Work the dough together with your hands until all of the flour is absorbed. Transfer to a well-floured board and knead the dough until it is no longer sticky, adding small amounts of flour if necessary as you knead.

Leave the dough on the floured board, cover, and let rise until at least doubled in bulk. Punch down, turn out onto another floured board, and roll until about ¾-inch thick. Cut into 4-inch squares and deep fry, a few at a time, in hot oil until golden brown. Place on paper towels to drain. Sprinkle both sides with additional salt to taste and rub with the garlic. Serve warm. Makes about 1½ dozen.

COCKAMAMY CHICKEN SALAD

1 large red apple, diced
¾ cup seedless raisins
1½ cups cooked diced
  chicken

1½ cups sliced celery
⅓ cup mayonnaise
1½ tbsp. lemon juice

Combine the apple, raisins, chicken, and celery. Mix well. Blend the mayonnaise and lemon juice together and stir lightly into the salad mixture. Serves 4 to 6.

PESHA'S PECAN SOUP

5 tsp. pareve beef soup mix
6 cups boiling water
2 cups pecan halves
1 stick pareve margarine
2 tbsp. finely chopped
   shallots or green onions
1 clove garlic, pressed

2 tbsp. tomato paste
1 tbsp. cornstarch, dissolved
   in ¼ cup water
1 egg yolk
¼ cup nondairy creamer, at
   room temperature
¼ tsp. white pepper
⅛ tsp. nutmeg

Dissolve the soup mix in the boiling water. Grind the pecans in a blender, and add them to the soup mix. Melt the pareve margarine in a 3-quart saucepan. Add the shallots and cook for 5 minutes until soft, but not brown. Add the garlic and cook 1 minute; then slowly add the nut mixture, tomato paste, and dissolved cornstarch. Cook for 30 minutes. Beat the egg yolk into the nondairy creamer; then slowly whisk them into the soup. Do not boil. Season with pepper and nutmeg. Serves 8.

SUMMER SOUTHERN SOUP
(Microwave and Conventional)

4 cups chicken broth
1 carrot, sliced
1 onion, diced
2 sprigs parsley
¼ tsp. oregano
2 ears corn or 1 8-oz. can
   whole kernel corn, drained
1½ cups cauliflower florets

1 cup fresh green beans, cut
   into 1-inch pieces
1 medium zucchini, sliced
2 tomatoes, cut into chunks
salt and freshly ground
   pepper to taste
chopped parsley

MICROWAVE: Combine the chicken broth, carrot, onion, parsley, and oregano in a 3-quart microwavable soup tureen or casserole. Cover tightly with plastic wrap, turning back one edge to vent. Microwave at 100% power for 6 minutes.

Cut the kernels from the ears of corn. Add the corn kernels, cauliflower, and green beans to the soup. Cover, leaving a vent, and cook at 100% power for 10 minutes. Add the zucchini and tomatoes; then cover and cook at 100% power for 5 minutes. Season to taste with salt and pepper. Ladle into soup bowls and sprinkle with chopped parsley. Serves 6.

CONVENTIONAL: Combine the chicken broth, carrot, onion, parsley, and oregano in a large saucepan; then heat to boiling. Reduce the heat, cover, and simmer for 10 minutes. Cut the kernels from the ears of corn; then add the corn, cauliflower, and green beans to the soup. Cover and simmer for 12 minutes. Stir in the zucchini and tomatoes and simmer for 5 minutes. Season to taste with salt and pepper. Ladle into soup bowls and sprinkle with chopped parsley. Serves 6.

BROCCOLI A-LA-BAMA

1 10-oz. pkg. frozen broccoli
2 tbsp. butter
1 tsp. salt
⅛ tsp. pepper
1 tbsp. flour

1 tbsp. prepared mustard
1 egg yolk, beaten
¾ cup milk
2 tsp. lemon juice

Cook the broccoli according to the package directions and drain. Melt the butter in a saucepan; then stir in the salt, pepper, and flour. Combine the mustard, egg yolk, and milk; then stir them into the flour mixture. Cook for 5 minutes, stirring constantly, until thickened. Stir in the lemon juice. Pour the sauce over the hot broccoli. Serves 3 to 4.

BATTLEFIELD BEANS

2 10-oz. pkg. French cut
  frozen green beans
4 tbsp. pareve margarine
1 medium onion, chopped
2 tsp. pareve beef flavored
  soup mix

2 tbsp. water
2 tbsp. sugar
2 tsp. prepared mustard
½ tsp. salt
¼ tsp. pepper

Cook the beans until tender; then drain. Melt the margarine in a saucepan; then cook the onions until glossy. Dissolve the soup mix in the 2 tablespoons of water. Add the sugar, prepared mustard, salt, pepper, and dissolved soup mix. Blend well until mixed; then add the cooked beans and simmer for 10 minutes more until flavor is absorbed into the beans. Serves 8 to 10.

YOLANDE'S YELLOW SQUASH

2 tbsp. butter
½ cup chopped yellow onion
2 large tomatoes, peeled,
  chopped, and drained
1 tsp. sugar
2¼ lb. yellow squash, sliced

1 tsp. salt
½ tsp. black pepper
⅛ tsp. Tabasco sauce
½ cup grated parmesan
  cheese

In a large skillet, melt the butter; then sauté the onion until it is limp, about 5 minutes. Add the tomatoes and sugar and cook for 10 minutes. Reduce the heat; then add the squash and salt. Cover and cook until tender. Season with pepper and Tabasco sauce. Pour into a 1½-quart shallow baking dish. Top with cheese; then broil until brown, about 10 minutes. Serves 6 to 8.

BAR MITZVAH BRUNCH FISH
(Microwave and Conventional)

1 lb. frozen fish fillets
4 tbsp. lemon juice, divided
Salt and freshly ground
  pepper
1 large tomato, peeled and
  diced

1 small ripe avocado, peeled
  and diced
2 shallots, sliced
4 slices toast
¼ cup sour cream
½ tsp. grated lemon peel

MICROWAVE: Cut partially thawed fish into 4 portions, and place them in an 8-inch round glass cake dish. Sprinkle with 2 tablespoons of the lemon juice and season with salt and pepper. Mix the tomato, avocado, and shallots with 1 tablespoon of the lemon juice; then spoon the mixture over the fish. Cover tightly with plastic wrap, turning back edge to vent. Microwave at 100% power for 6 to 8 minutes, until fish flakes easily. Let stand, covered, for 5 minutes; then lift the fish from the baking dish with a slotted spatula. Place on toast. Combine the sour cream, lemon peel, and remaining tablespoon of lemon juice; then spoon it over the fish. Serves 4.

CONVENTIONAL: Preheat the oven to 350°. Cut the partially thawed fish into 4 portions, and place them in an 8-inch baking dish. Sprinkle with 2 tablespoons of the lemon juice and season with salt and pepper. Combine the tomato, avocado, shallots, and 1 tablespoon of the lemon juice; then spoon the mixture over the fish. Bake for 20 minutes or until the fish flakes easily. Lift the fish from the baking dish with a slotted spatula. Place on toast. Combine the sour cream, lemon peel, and the remaining tablespoon of lemon juice; then spoon it over the fish. Serves 4.

COQUETTE CASSEROLE

½ lb. mushrooms, sliced
3 tbsp. butter or margarine, divided
1½ tbsp. lemon juice
½ cup Kosher white wine
⅛ tsp. dried thyme
1 bay leaf

¼ tsp. salt
dash pepper
½ lb. fish fillets, sliced in 2-inch pieces
1 tbsp. flour
½ cup heavy cream
1 cup buttered bread crumbs

Sauté the mushrooms in 2 tablespoons of the butter and the lemon juice until tender. Combine the wine, seasonings, and fish in a saucepan and simmer for 5 minutes. In a separate saucepan, melt the remaining tablespoon of butter; then stir in the flour and cook, stirring, for 2 minutes. Remove from the heat to add the cream; then bring the sauce quickly to a boil. Remove from heat and combine the mushrooms, fish, and sauce; then pour into individual casseroles. Sprinkle with the buttered bread crumbs. Bake at 400° for about 10 minutes until browned. Serves 4.

PINSK FISH PLATTER
(Microwave)

4 carrots, cut in 2x⅛-inch strips
2 stalks celery, cut in 1-inch slices
2 tbsp. water
parsley flakes
salt to taste

2 tbsp. butter
8 to 12 oz. defrosted flounder fillets
4 tsp. lemon juice
½ tsp. paprika
2 tbsp. sliced shallots
4 tbsp. almonds, toasted

Place carrot strips around the edge of a microwave-safe platter. Top with the celery, water, parsley and salt. Dice 2 teaspoons of the butter and place it on the vegetables. Cover with plastic wrap, turning back one edge to vent. Microwave on high power for 2 minutes. Uncover and place the fish in the center of the platter. Top with lemon juice, remaining butter, paprika, and shallots. Cover with plastic wrap, leaving one edge open to vent, and microwave on high power 2 minutes. Let stand 2 minutes; then sprinkle with toasted almonds. Serves 2.

VULCAN VEAL
(Microwave)

½ cup dry seasoned bread crumbs
¾ tsp. dill weed
1 egg, beaten
2 tsp. lemon juice

4 veal cutlets (about 1 lb.)
2 tbsp. pareve margarine
1 cup sliced fresh mushrooms
¼ cup chopped onions

On a sheet of waxed paper, combine the bread crumbs and dill weed. Set aside. Blend the egg and lemon juice together in a shallow bowl; then dip the cutlets into the egg mixture and dredge in the bread crumbs.

Preheat a 10-inch browning dish in the microwave on high for 5 minutes. Quickly add the pareve margarine and the breaded veal. Microwave on high for 45 seconds; then turn, add the mushrooms and onions, and cover. Microwave on high for 4 to 6 minutes, until the veal and vegetables are fork-tender. Rearrange the cutlets after the first 2 minutes. Serves 4.

CHICK-A-STEW

1 3-lb. fryer chicken
1 onion minced
2½ cups cooked corn
1 8-oz. can tomato sauce
1 tsp. Worcestershire sauce
1 tbsp. ketchup
dash Tabasco sauce

½ tsp. salt
⅛ tsp. pepper
1 15-oz. can green lima beans
2 medium potatoes, diced
1 tsp. lemon juice
¼ cup pareve margarine

Place the chicken in a saucepan and cover it with water. Add the onion; then bring it to a boil. Reduce the heat to simmer until the chicken is tender. Remove the chicken from the broth and allow it to cool. Remove the chicken meat from the bones and place it back into the broth. Add the remaining ingredients and simmer for 1 hour, stirring frequently. Serves 4.

CAVALRY KRAUT
(Microwave)

1 medium apple, chopped
½ cup chopped onion
1 cup chopped celery
1 16-oz. can sauerkraut,
  drained
1 8-oz. can crushed
  pineapple, drained

2 tsp. sugar
1 tsp. cornstarch
1 tsp. salt
⅛ tsp. garlic powder
⅛ tsp. pepper
8 wieners, cut in fourths

Combine the apple, onion, and celery in a 2-quart casserole. Cover and microwave on high for 3 to 5 minutes, until the celery is tender. Stir in the remaining ingredients, except the wieners. Add the wieners and push them to the bottom of the casserole so they are covered with the sauerkraut mixture. Cover. Microwave for 6 to 9 minutes, until thoroughly heated, stirring at the halfway point. Serves 4.

'BAMA SHORT RIBS

2 medium onions
4 lb. beef chuck short ribs
1 tsp. salt
water
1 medium green pepper
2 tbsp. salad oil
1 clove garlic, crushed

¾ cup ketchup
2 tbsp. brown sugar
½ tsp. Worchestershire sauce
½ tsp. Tabasco sauce
⅓ cup water
¼ tsp. salt

Cut one onion into quarters. Set aside the remaining onion. In a 6-quart dutch oven over high heat, heat the chuck short ribs, the quartered onion, 1 teaspoon of the salt and enough water to cover everything. Bring to a boil; then reduce the heat to low, cover, and simmer for 1¼ hours, until the meat is fork-tender. Remove the ribs to a platter.

Dice the green pepper and the reserved onion. In a 2-quart saucepan, heat the salad oil until hot. Cook the green pepper, onion, and garlic over medium heat until tender, stirring occasionally. Stir in the ketchup, brown sugar, Worchestershire sauce, Tabasco sauce, ⅓ cup water, and ¼ teaspoon salt over high heat. Heat to boiling. Reduce heat to low, cover, and simmer for 5 minutes to blend the flavors.

Preheat the broiler. Arrange the ribs on a rack in a broiler pan, about 5 inches from the heat. Broil the ribs for 20 minutes until they are heated through, brushing them with sauce and turning them occasionally. Serves 6.

BIRMING "HAM"

1 7- to 8-lb. fully cooked corn beef
1 8-oz. jar red maraschino cherries
1 cup brown sugar, firmly packed
½ cup orange juice
½ tsp. whole cloves
2 medium oranges, sliced and halved
parsley

Place the corn beef in a baking pan. Bake at 325° for 30 to 40 minutes, or until the meat is heated through and tender enough to score.

Drain the cherries, reserving the syrup. Combine the brown sugar, reserved cherry syrup, orange juice, and whole cloves in a saucepan. Cook, stirring occasionally, until slightly thickened.

Remove the corn beef from the oven; then score it and decorate with cherries and orange slices secured with toothpicks. Brush it with the glaze mixture and bake for 30 minutes, brushing frequently with the glaze. Place the corn beef on a platter and garnish with parsley. Serves 10.

BLACKBERRY JAM CAKE

2 cups sifted flour
1 tsp. baking powder
1 tsp. baking soda
1 tsp. cinnamon
2 cups sugar
1 cup blackberry jam
3 eggs, beaten
1 cup plumped raisins
1 cup buttermilk
1 cup chopped pecans
1 7-oz. pkg. flaked coconut

Sift the flour, baking powder, baking soda, cinnamon, and sugar together in a bowl. Combine the remaining ingredients and mix; then mix in the flour mixture. Turn into three waxed-paper lined and greased 9-inch layer cake pans. Bake at 350 degrees for 30 to 40 minutes, until cake tests done.

Icing

4 tbsp. flour
1½ cups evaporated milk
1½ cups sugar
1 cup flaked coconut

¼ cup blackberry jam
1 cup butter
1 cup chopped nuts

Mix the flour with a small amount of the milk to make a smooth paste; then combine it with the remaining ingredients in a saucepan. Cook, stirring constantly, until it is of spreading consistency. Spread the icing between the layers and over the sides and top of the cake. Ices one 3-layer 9-inch cake.

FINGER LICKIN' FUDGE

¼ lb. unsweetened chocolate
2 tbsp. butter
¾ cup half-and-half
2 cups sugar

3½ tbsp. corn syrup
⅛ tsp. salt
1 tsp. vanilla extract

Butter an 8-inch or 9-inch square baking pan. Chop the chocolate into small pieces and cut the butter into chunks. Combine the half-and-half, sugar, corn syrup, and salt in a heavy saucepan. Cook over low heat, stirring occasionally, for about 10 minutes until sugar dissolves. Do not boil. Stir in the chopped chocolate. Let simmer for about 30 minutes, without stirring, over very low heat until a candy thermometer registers 234°. Remove from heat; then add the butter chunks and let them melt without stirring. Let the mixture stand for about 30 minutes until thermometer registers 150°. Add the vanilla; then beat the mixture for about 5 minutes until it starts to lose its gloss but is still soft. Pour into the prepared pan. Let stand until firm, at least 2 hours. Cut into pieces about 1½-inches by 2 inches. Makes 20 pieces.

CRIMSON TIDE CHOCOLATE PIE
(Microwave)

2 cups Kosher miniature
 marshmallows
1 cup milk chocolate morsels
1 cup milk
1 1-oz. square unsweetened
 chocolate

1 cup whipping cream,
 whipped
Chocolate Crust

Combine the marshmallows, chocolate morsels, milk, and unsweetened chocolate in a 2-quart glass mixing bowl. Microwave on high for 4 to 5 minutes, stirring once. Cool. Fold in the whipped cream, and pour into the prepared Chocolate Crust. Freeze until firm. Makes on 9-inch pie.

Chocolate Crust

⅓ cup butter or margarine
1½ cups chocolate wafer crumbs

Place the butter in a small glass mixing bowl. Microwave on high for 50 seconds. Add the chocolate crumbs and mix well. Press the chocolate crumb mixture into a 9-inch pie plate. Microwave on high for 1 minute or until firm. Cool. Makes one 9-inch chocolate wafer crust.

DECATUR DEEP DISH PIE

1⅓ cups all-purpose flour
2 tbsp. sugar
¼ tsp. salt
½ cup cold unsalted butter, cut into bits
1 large egg yolk, beaten
1½ tbsp. ice water
3 tbsp. cornstarch
3 tbsp. water
1 tbsp. lemon juice
⅔ cup sugar
¼ tsp. cinnamon
8 cups blueberries, picked over
1 egg
2 tsp. water
1½ tbsp. sugar

In a large bowl, stir together the flour, sugar, and salt; then add the butter and blend the mixture until it resembles coarse meal. Beat the egg yolk with the 1½ tablespoons of water; then add it to the flour mixture and toss until the liquid is incorporated. Form the dough into a ball. Dust the dough with flour and chill, wrapped in a plastic wrap, for 1 hour.

In a large bowl, stir together the cornstarch, water, lemon juice, sugar, and cinnamon. Add the blueberries and stir the mixture well. Pour the filling into a 6 to 7-cup baking dish.

On a floured surface, roll out the dough to slightly larger than the size of dish. Drape it over the filling. Fold the overhanging dough under, pressing it to the edge of the dish. Crimp the edge decoratively. Make slits or holes in the crust for air vents. Beat the remaining egg, water, and sugar together; then brush the crust with the egg wash, and sprinkle it with extra sugar. Bake the pie on a baking sheet in the middle of a preheated 375° oven for 1 to 1¼ hours, or until the filling is bubbly and the crust is golden. Transfer the baked pie to a rack to let it cool before serving. Serves 8.

GEORGIA
The Empire State of the South

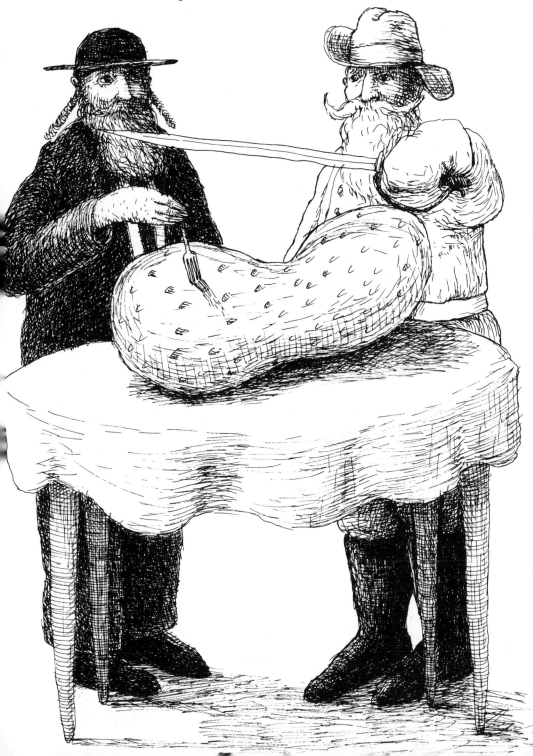

Long before the white man came to North America, the region that is now Georgia was occupied by the civilized and peace-loving Cherokee and Creek Indians.

Hernando De Soto, a Spaniard, was lured on his extended expedition by tales of wealth in the New World. He passed through Georgia on his way to the Mississippi River around the year 1540. As a result, the territory was claimed by Spain. At the same time, the French and English explorers were also seeking to establish their claims and to control the entire continent.

By the mid-1600s, the territory was claimed by England. In 1732, George II, for whom the state was named, granted a charter to a group of wealthy Englishman headed by General James E. Oglethorpe. Under this charter, they planned to establish a colony as a haven for the debtors who were crowding English prisons and the Protestants who were persecuted in Germany and Austria. Additionally, the colony was to serve as a defense buffer against the Spaniards in Florida and the French in Louisiana. Georgia became the last of the original thirteen English colonies to be formally settled.

The years following the Revolution saw rapid industrial and agricultural growth of the state, earning its nickname, The Empire State of the South. Georgia was, and still is, the largest state east of the Mississippi River. However, Georgia is better known as The Cracker State. The Crackers were the early white impoverished rural settlers who lived in Georgia prior to the Civil War.

Georgia settlers cultivated numerous crops for England, but the colony failed to thrive economically because of the warm climate and the prohibition of slaves. To save the colony, Oglethorpe and his trustees reversed their original position, and allowed the introduction of slaves into Georgia in 1749.

Slavery manpower enabled Georgia to successfully cultivate all her crops. Thanks to Eli Whitney's invention of the cotton gin, farmers were able to separate the cotton from the seed, and the production of cotton increased significantly. After this invention, residents could turn their attention to commerce. Because of the state's economic dependence on slave labor, Georgia felt that the federal government had no right to prohibit slavery. After Abraham Lincoln was elected president, Georgia seceded from the Union. The act of secession was adopted on January 19, 1861, making Georgia the fifth state to secede.

During the war, Georgia became a center of both triumphant victories and dispiriting defeats. At Chickamauga on September 19 and 20, 1863, the first great battle fought in Georgia would become known as the two bloodiest days of the war. The war dragged on, and in 1864, General William T. Sherman began his famous march through Georgia. Those were dark and bloody days. Atlanta, and all of Georgia, seemed to be in flames. Unfortunately, there were few Rhett Butler's and Scarlett O'Hara's to romanticize or lessen the toll of the war. Georgia suffered more damage than most of the other southern states. About one hundred million dollars worth of property was destroyed by Sherman's forces as he marched through the state.

With the silencing of guns came the hard times. The Reconstruction policy did little to improve conditions, but Georgia rose from its own ashes, "never to go hungry again." With a strong sense of pride and determination, Georgia gradually began to rebuild, and proceeded into the twentieth century with optimism. Prosperity continued during the two world wars and into the postwar years. Georgia witnessed a historic revitalization as well as economic success. The Empire State of the South became a mecca for tourists and history buffs, and an attractive site for major industries.

It is difficult to believe that it all began in 1733, when the Yamacraw Indians shared a bountiful feast with General James E. Oglethorpe and his fellow British settlers. This meal marked the beginning of the state as well as the beginning of a cuisine that is unique to Georgia. French, German, Scottish, and English settlers brought with them their Old World ways and recipes. The frontier women, the slaves, and the Crackers added their influences to the Old World recipes; and eventually they adapted together to the land and its produce. What emerged would reflect a culinary combination of past and present.

Today, Georgia serves almost anything your taste buds desire, from fresh seafood to gourmet cuisine. Take your taste buds on a historic and culinary tour of Georgia. With the wonderful aromas of southern fare wafting through the air amidst antebellum grandeur, you will forever have "Georgia on [your] mind."

BEEF WITH CELERY,
AND WHITE BEANS AND PEAS

Soak for twelve hours one pint of dried white peas, and a half pint of the same kind of beans, they must be well soaked, and if very dry, may require longer than twelve hours, put a nice piece of brisket of about eight pounds weight, in a stew pan with the peas and beans, and three heads of celery cut in small pieces; put water enough to cover, and season with pepper and salt only; let it all stew slowly till the meat is extremely tender and the peas and beans quite soft, then add four large lumps of sugar and nearly a teacup of vinegar; this is a very fine stew.

DE BES' DAIQUIRIS

1 10-oz. pkg. frozen peaches, partially thawed	½ 6-oz. can frozen lemonade concentrate
6 oz. light rum	2 cups crushed ice

Combine all ingredients and whirl in a blender until the peaches are pureed and the mixture is uniform. Store in a covered plastic container in the freezer until you are ready to serve. Thaw slightly and spoon into small cocktail glasses. Serves 8 to 10.

SCARLETT'S SYLLABUB

1 cup fresh sliced peaches	1 cup whipping cream
1 tbsp. lemon juice	1 egg white
⅝ cup powdered sugar	2 tbsp. sherry

Combine the peaches, lemon juice, and 2 tablespoons of the sugar in a bowl and set it aside. Whip the cream with ¼ cup of the sugar until stiff. Beat the egg white with the remaining sugar until stiff; then fold it into the whipped cream. Add the sherry and pour it over the peaches. Serves 4.

OH! HARA'S HOE CAKE

1 tsp. salt
2 cups cornmeal
½ to ¾ cups water

2 tbsp. Beef Frye drippings, divided

Add the salt to the cornmeal, then add the water and 1 tablespoon of the Beef Frye drippings. Heat the remaining tablespoon of drippings in a heavy iron skillet. Make a round cake out of the cornmeal dough about 1 to 1½ inches thick. Place in the hot skillet and cook slowly until brown on one side, then turn and brown the other side. Serve hot. Serves 4 to 6.

PRISSY'S PEANUT SOUP

2 tbsp. pareve margarine
2 tbsp. grated onion
1 rib celery, sliced thin
2 tbsp. flour
3 cups chicken broth

½ cup creamy peanut butter
¼ tsp. salt
2 tsp. lemon juice
2 tbsp. chopped roasted peanuts

Melt the pareve margarine in a saucepan over low heat; then add the onion and celery. Sauté for about 5 minutes. Add the flour and mix until well blended. Stir in the chicken broth and allow it to simmer for about 30 minutes.

Remove from heat, and strain the broth. Stir the peanut butter, salt, and lemon juice into the strained broth until well mixed. Serve hot in cups, garnished with a teaspoon of chopped peanuts. Serves 6.

PEACHIE SOUP

1 pint water
⅛ tsp. cinnamon
2 whole cloves

2 cups sliced peaches
2 cups white wine
sugar to taste

Combine the water, spices, and peaches in a saucepan and simmer until the peaches are tender. Press them through a colander. Stir the wine and sugar into the liquid and heat just to the boiling point. Remove from the heat and chill. Serve in bouillon cups. (Apple cider or grape juice may be substituted for the wine.) Serves 6.

SHERMAN'S SLAW-TER

4 cups shredded cabbage
1 large carrot, shredded
½ cup chopped celery
¾ cup mayonnaise
¼ cup fresh lemon juice

2 tsp. sugar
½ tsp. dry mustard
½ tsp. Worcestershire sauce
⅛ tsp. Tabasco sauce
salt and pepper to taste

In a large bowl, toss together the cabbage, carrots, and celery. Set aside. In a small bowl, combine the mayonnaise, lemon juice, sugar, mustard, Worcestershire sauce, and Tabasco sauce. Toss to coat; then add salt and pepper to taste. Chill until serving time. Makes 4 cups.

GEFILTE FISH PIE

8 medium potatoes, diced
1 medium onion, chopped
2 cups diced carrots
1 cup chopped celery
water
½ tsp. salt
4 large gefilte fish balls, cut
  into ¼-inch by 2-inch
  pieces

4 hard-cooked eggs
½ tsp. pepper
½ cup pareve margarine
1 prepared double pie crust
  dough, chilled

Preheat the oven to 450 degrees. Place the potatoes, onion, carrots, and celery in a large pot and cover them with water. Add the salt and cover. Bring to a boil and cook over medium heat for 20 minutes. Add the gefilte fish pieces.

Using a slotted spoon, immediately remove the contents from pot and place them in a 9x13-inch baking pan. Add enough liquid from pot to almost cover the fish and vegetables. Slice the eggs and place them over the top. Sprinkle with pepper and dot with pareve margarine.

Roll the chilled pie dough into a rectangle large enough to cover the ingredients in the pan. Seal the edges and prick at intervals with a fork.

Bake the pie for 10 minutes at 450 degrees. Turn oven to 350 degrees and continue baking for approximately 1 hour, or until the crust has browned evenly. Serves 6 to 8.

SAVANNAH SWAMP FISH & GRAVY

3 lb. fish fillets
1½ tbsp. salt

1 cup cornmeal
vegetable oil for deep frying

Sprinkle the fish with salt and coat them with cornmeal. Fry in hot oil until brown. Drain on absorbent paper. Serves 6.

Gravy

½ cup vegetable oil
1 tbsp. cornmeal
3 cups diced potatoes
1 cup diced onion
1 cup tomato juice

2½ cups canned tomatoes, with liquid
1 tsp. salt
1 tsp. pepper

Pour the vegetable oil into a saucepan. Add the cornmeal, potatoes, and onion; then cook until tender. Add the remaining ingredients and cook, stirring frequently, until thickened. Serve with fish fillets.

TARA TUNA

2 cups cooked rice, cooled
1 6½-oz. can tuna, drained and flaked
2 tsp. minced parsley
½ tsp. Worcestershire sauce

1 egg, separated
1 tbsp. water
½ cup dry bread crumbs
oil for frying

Combine the rice, tuna, parsley, Worcestershire sauce, and egg yolk. Shape the mixture into 6 croquettes. Add the water to the egg white and beat slightly. Dip the croquettes in the egg white mixture, drain, and coat with the bread crumbs. Let the coating dry for a few minutes. Deep fry in oil heated to 365 degrees for 2½ to 3 minutes, or until golden brown. Drain on absorbent paper. Serves 6.

'LANTA'S LAMB CHOPS
(Microwave)

1 small onion, chopped
1 tbsp. pareve margarine
¼ cup chili sauce
¼ cup catsup

3 tbsp. brown sugar
1 tsp. vinegar
⅛ tsp. garlic powder
4 lamb chops (1½ inch thick)

In a 1-quart casserole, combine the onion and pareve margarine. Microwave on high for 1½ to 2 minutes, or until tender. Stir in the remaining ingredients, except the lamb chops.

Arrange the chops on a roasting rack with meatiest portions to the outside. Spoon half of the sauce over the chops; then cover with waxed paper. Microwave on high for 3 minutes. Reduce the power to 50% (medium), and microwave for 5 minutes. Turn over and rearrange the chops, spoon on the remaining sauce; then cover. Microwave for 10 to 20 minutes, until the chops are the desired doneness. Serves 4.

MAVEN'S MEAT CHOPS

6 veal chops, cut 1-inch thick
salt and pepper to taste
1 5-oz. pkg. yellow rice mix

1 cup chopped onions
1 14½-oz. can tomatoes,
   drained and chopped
   (reserve liquid)

Season the veal chops with salt and pepper. Place them in a skillet and brown on each side. Remove from the skillet and pour off the excess fat. Add the rice, onions, and tomatoes to the skillet. Combine the reserved liquid from the tomatoes with enough water to make 1⅔ cups liquid. Stir the liquid into the rice mixture and bring to a boil. Place the chops on top of the rice mixture. Reduce the heat, cover, and simmer for 15 minutes, until the rice is tender and the liquid is absorbed. Serves 6.

JOHNNY REBS CHICKEN

2 whole chicken breasts,
boned and skinned
1 egg, slightly beaten
1 tbsp. water
¾ cups finely chopped
pecans
2 tbsp. pareve margarine
2 cups sliced mushrooms

1½ cups water
2 tsp. instant chicken soup
mix
1 tbsp. cornstarch
1 tsp. spicy brown mustard
½ cup shallots with tops
2 tbsp. chopped parsley
2 tbsp. chopped pimiento

Split the breasts into cutlets by cutting them in half horizontally. Beat egg and water together in a pie plate. Place the pecans in a second pie plate. Coat chicken on both sides first in egg, then in pecans. Over medium heat, brown the chicken in the pareve margarine. Add the mushrooms, 1¼ cups of the water, and the dry soup mix. Bring to boil; then reduce the heat and simmer, covered, for 20 minutes or until the chicken is tender.

Blend the remaining ¼ cup of water with the cornstarch until dissolved. Stir it into the sauce and cook, stirring, until smooth and thickened. Add the mustard, shallots, parsley, and pimiento. Heat thoroughly. Serves 4.

FRENCHIE'S FRIED ONION RINGS

¾ cup sifted all-purpose flour
¼ tsp. salt
½ cup milk
2 tbsp. vegetable oil

1 egg
3 medium-sized Vidalia
onions, peeled
vegetable oil for deep frying

Sift the flour and salt into a bowl. Add the milk, oil, and egg; then beat until smooth. Cut the onions into ¼-inch-thick slices and separate them into rings. Dip each ring into the batter, draining the excess batter over the bowl. Drop, a few at a time, into deep oil heated to 375 degrees. Fry for 2 to 3 minutes turning occasionally. Drain on absorbent paper. Serves 4 to 5.

GEORGIA CRACKER CABBAGE
(Microwave and Conventional)

¼ large head cabbage, thinly
   sliced
1 apple, quartered and sliced
   ¼-inch-thick
⅓ cup raisins

½ cup orange juice
1 tsp. cornstarch
2 tsp. Worcestershire sauce
¼ tsp. salt
¼ tsp. garlic salt

CONVENTIONAL: Arrange the cabbage, apple slices, and raisins on a steamer rack over hot water in a dutch oven. Cover and cook over high heat for 5 to 7 minutes, or until cabbage is tender.

Meanwhile, mix together the orange juice, cornstarch, Worcestershire sauce, salt, and garlic salt. Remove the steamer containing the cabbage and fruits and discard the water. Pour the orange juice mixture into a pan and heat until thickened. Add the cabbage, apples, and raisins; then stir to coat. Serves 4 to 6.

MICROWAVE: Combine orange juice, cornstarch, Worcestershire sauce, salt, and garlic salt in a 1-cup glass bowl. Microwave on high for 1 to 2 minutes, stirring once or twice, until thickened. Set aside. Combine the sliced cabbage, apple slices, and raisins in a 3-quart casserole. Cover with vented plastic wrap and microwave on high for 4 to 6 minutes, stirring after 3 minutes, until the cabbage is tender. Drain the cabbage; then stir in the cooked sauce. Microwave for 2 to 3 minutes or until hot. Serves 4 to 6.

OLIVIA'S ONION CASSEROLE

1 11-oz. pkg. shelled black-
eyed peas (about 2½ cups)
2 cups water
2 medium Vidalia onions,
chopped
2 large cloves garlic, minced
½ cup chopped celery
2 tsp. Worcestershire sauce
Salt and black pepper to taste
⅛ tsp. Tabasco sauce
½ lb. Kosher pastrami

Place the peas, water, onions, garlic, celery, Worcestershire sauce, salt, pepper, and Tabasco sauce in a 3-quart microwave-safe casserole and stir. Add the pastrami. Cover and microwave on high for 40 to 50 minutes, or until peas are tender. Stir every 10 minutes, and add more water if necessary during cooking. Let stand for 5 minutes; then drain. Remove the meat and cut it into small pieces. Add the meat to the peas and mix well. Adjust seasoning if necessary. Serves 6.

UNCLE TOM'S TOMATOES

2 slices Beef Frye
1 large onion, chopped
1 medium green pepper,
chopped
1 lb. okra, sliced
1 lb. peeled tomatoes,
chopped
1 tsp. salt
½ tsp. pepper

Fry the Beef Frye in a heavy skillet until brown and crisp; then remove it from the skillet. Sauté the onion and green pepper in the Beef Frye drippings until tender. Add the remaining ingredients; then crumble the Beef Frye and add it to the okra mixture. Cover and cook for 30 to 35 minutes. Uncover and cook for 5 minutes. Serves 6.

YAMACRAW YAMS
(Microwave)

¼ cup butter
¼ cup all-purpose flour
½ tsp. salt
⅛ tsp. cinnamon
dash nutmeg
1 cup milk
¼ cup brown sugar

1 cup mashed, cooked sweet
  potatoes
4 eggs, separated
1 tsp. cream of tartar
2 tbsp. chopped unsalted
peanuts

In a 2-quart casserole, microwave the butter on high for 30 to 45 seconds, or until melted. Blend in the flour and seasonings; then slowly stir in the milk. Microwave on high for 3 to 3½ minutes, stirring every minute, until thickened. Add the brown sugar, sweet potatoes, and slightly beaten egg yolks.

In a large mixing bowl, beat the egg whites with the cream of tartar until stiff peaks form. Gently fold the egg whites into the thickened sauce. Microwave at 50% (medium) for 15 to 19 minutes, or until the top edges appear dry and the center seems set. Rotate ¼ turn about every 3 minutes. Sprinkle with peanuts. Serves 3 to 4.

THE V.P.'S PEANUT PIE

4 eggs separated
2 tbsp. butter
2 cups sugar
1 cup raisins

1 cup crushed unsalted
  peanuts
3 tsp. lemon juice
1 tsp. vanilla extract
1 unbaked 9-inch pie shell

Beat the egg yolks until light. Cream the butter and sugar together; then add the egg yolks. Stir in the raisins, peanuts, lemon juice, and vanilla. Mix well. Lightly beat the egg whites; then fold them in. Pour into the pie shell and bake at 325 degrees for 50 minutes. Serves 8.

DOWN HOME "BROITE" PUDDING

1 8-oz. pkg. cream cheese
⅔ cup sugar
4 eggs
1 cup milk
½ tsp. almond extract
1 tsp. grated lemon peel
1 tsp. vanilla

3½ cups dry ½-inch bread
  cubes
1 29-oz. can peach halves
3 tbsp. seedless raspberry jam
4 tsp. sugar
¼ tsp. ground cinnamon
¼ cup sliced almonds

In a mixer bowl, beat the cream cheese and ⅔ cup sugar with an electric mixer on medium speed until smooth. Add the eggs; then beat until well blended. On low speed, beat in the milk, almond extract, lemon peel, and vanilla.

Place the bread cubes in a greased 12x7½x2-inch baking dish. Pour the egg mixture over the bread. Place the peach halves, cut side up, on top of the egg mixture. (Do not allow the egg mixture to flow into the center of the peach halves.) Spoon 1 teaspoon of jam into each peach center. Combine the remaining sugar and the cinnamon; then sprinkle it over peaches. Top with sliced almonds. Bake in a 325-degree oven for 40 to 45 minutes, until set. Cool slightly. Serve warm with raspberry sauce. Serves 8.

RAISEL'S RASPBERRY SAUCE

1 10-oz. pkg. frozen red
  raspberries
2 tbsp. sugar

2 tsp. cornstarch
1 tbsp. seedless raspberry jam
1 tsp. lemon juice

Thaw the package of frozen red raspberries. Sieve to remove the seeds. Discard the seeds. In a small saucepan, combine the sugar and cornstarch; then add to the raspberry mixture. Cook, stirring until thickened and bubbly. Cook 1 minute more; then remove from heat. Stir in the raspberry jam and lemon juice. Makes 1 cup.

AUNTEE BELLUM'S SORBET

1¼ lb. fresh peaches, peeled, pitted and chopped (about 2½ cups)
3 tbsp. lemon juice
1 cup sugar
1 cup boiling water
1 cup white wine
1½ tsp. grated orange peel
Long, thin strips of orange peel
1 cup fresh raspberries

In a blender or food processor bowl, combine the peaches and lemon juice. Cover and process until smooth. In a large mixing bowl, stir together the sugar and boiling water, until sugar is dissolved. Stir in the peach mixture, wine, and grated orange peel; then pour into a 9x9x2-inch pan. Cover and freeze for 3 to 4 hours until firm.

Break into chunks and transfer to a chilled, large mixer bowl. Beat with an electric mixer on medium-high speed until smooth. Return to pan. Cover and freeze for several hours until firm. Let stand for 15 to 20 minutes at room temperature before scooping into dessert dishes. Serve with orange peel strips and raspberries. Serves 8.

POW WOW PUDDIN'

½ cup white hominy grits
¼ tsp. salt
2⅓ cups water
⅓ cup sugar
1 tbsp. butter or margarine
3 eggs, beaten
1⅓ cups milk
1 tsp. vanilla
1 tsp. nutmeg
¼ cup raisins
¼ cup chopped peanuts

Prepare the grits in salted boiling water as directed on package. Stir in the sugar and butter. Combine the eggs, milk, vanilla, and nutmeg; then add to the grits. Pour the mixture into a greased 8-inch square baking dish. Sprinkle with raisins and peanuts. Bake in a preheated oven at 325 degrees for about 50 minutes. Cut into squares and serve warm. Serves 6 to 8.

LOUISIANA
The Pelican State

History has a fascinating way of bringing people and places together. Certainly that has been the case with the state of Louisiana—a state that has its own unique heritage and culture. Its colorful and fascinating history began when Robert Cavalier de la Salle took possession of the Mississippi Valley in 1682. He named the territory Louisiana, for Louis XIV of France. From this origin came the establishment of a French colonial empire that continues to influence Louisiana to the present day.

During the French rule, Natchitoches, the first city in Louisiana, was founded. Four years later, in 1718, Jean Baptiste Le Moyne, Sieur de Bienville founded New Orleans. He named it for the Duc d'Orléans. Louisiana continued to grow as more and more people settled in the territory. Amongst those people were the first wave of Acadians—French Catholics exiled from Nova Scotia. These Acadians, known today as Cajuns, settled in southwestern Louisiana in 1760. Their culture has added much to the lifestyle of Louisiana.

Although the French influence was building in Louisiana, in 1762 King Louis XV ceded all of the territory west of the Mississippi, including the Isle of Orleans, to its ally, Spain. Many different people came to Louisiana, but none with more flourish and flamboyance than the Spanish. Their brilliant uniforms sparkled in the bright sun as 2600 soldiers marched in Jackson Square, the army post in New Orleans. The Spaniards came to administer, not to colonize, as the French had. They ruled harshly and sternly, which prompted the French colonists to revolt. The colonists were defeated and the French knew their rule, for the time being, had come to an end.

Napoleon, however, realized that Spain had overextended herself. Spain had recently conquered the British West Indies, including eastern Florida, and at the same time was ruling over Louisiana. The economic cost and necessary manpower for control of these newly acquired territories weakened Spain's coffers and military strength. Napoleon recognized this weakness and forced Spain to give the Louisiana colony back to France. For 21 days, once again, the French flag flew over Louisiana.

At the end of the three-week period, in 1803, Napoleon executed the Louisiana Purchase with the United States. At two-and-one-half cents an acre, totaling $15,000,000, it was the greatest real estate transaction in the history of the United States. With this purchase, the United States acquired an area three times greater than that of the original thirteen states. Settlers came from the Southeast to live in northern and central Louisiana. During this time, the territory of Orleans was renamed Louisiana. On April 8, 1812, Louisiana was admitted into the Union as the eighteenth state.

The temperament and customs of the people of Louisiana differed greatly from those in other sections of the country. In the southernmost part of Louisiana, a new generation of Creoles emerged. These were people of French or Spanish descent, born in America—the first native-born generation. Ambitious, enterprising, and educated, they added much to the cultural and economic growth of the territory. In the southwestern part of the state, the same could be said of the Cajuns. In the northernmost part, other immigrants settled in the rich farmlands.

The mid-1800s saw Louisiana develop as an important agricultural and commercial state. However, this prosperity and growth was soon shattered as the talk of war became a reality. On January 26, 1861, Louisiana passed the Ordinance of Secession, becoming the sixth state to join the newly formed Confederacy.

Louisiana suffered along with its sister states as the Civil War progressed. The port of New Orleans at the mouth of the Mississippi River was vital to the Confederacy. Trade, however, came to a standstill when Admiral David Glasgow Farragut, in 1862, boldly sailed up the Mississippi River, past Fort St. Philip and Fort Jackson, to defeat the Confederate flotilla, thus enabling the Union troops to capture New Orleans and Baton Rouge.

The state endured heavy losses and found itself virtually bankrupt at the end of the war. Reconstruction delayed its recovery further still. Louisiana limped along until the late 1800s, when foreign and domestic trade once again returned to the mouth of the Mississippi.

Since the early 1900s, Louisiana has made steady economical progress. The state is proud of its natural resources. It is a land of bayous and marshes that are still rich with wildlife. It is home to the pelican, the state bird which gave Louisiana its nickname, the Pelican State. It is loved by the sportsman, who often refers to Louisiana as Sportsman's Paradise.

Louisiana, which literally means "Land of Louis," has had a colorful and exciting history and produced equally colorful and exciting people: Jean Lafitte and his pirates; Madame Marie Laveau, the voodoo queen; Governor Huey P. Long, the political figure known as the "Kingfish"; trumpeter Louis Armstrong, world famous ambassador of good will; and, of course, Rex, the king of Mardi Gras.

Although time has changed us all, Louisianians have held fast, in their hearts and in their land, to certain elements of the past: the Indian arts and crafts, the Spanish architecture, the heritage of jazz music, and the French culinary influence that still dominates Louisiana's cuisine.

Tourists from all walks of life, and all parts of the world, come to Louisiana. Louisiana plays host to them all. Each and every one is invited to visit a state that offers everything from a tour of the original French seat of government, to the backroads of simple country life, to the Superdome. Your unforgettable trip begins as you climb aboard the "Louisiana Hayride."

TO MAKE PANCAKES

Take a pint of cream, and eight eggs, white and all, a whole nutmeg grated, and a little salt; then melt a pound of rare dish butter, and a little sack; before you fry them, stir it in; it must be made as thick with three spoonfuls of flour, as ordinary batter, and fry'd with butter in the pan, the first Pancake, but no more: Strew sugar, garnish with orange, turn it on the backside of the plate.

L'CHAIM COCKTAIL

1 lump sugar
1 tsp. water
½ lemon, juice only

1 jigger cherry brandy
1 jigger cognac
1 maraschino cherry

Dissolve sugar in water. Add the lemon juice and the two brandies. Stir with ice and strain into a cocktail glass. Drop in the cherry. Serves 1.

PADDLE WHEEL PUNCH

⅓ cup pineapple juice
⅓ cup orange juice
⅓ cup lime or lemon juice

1 tsp. grenadine syrup
2 jiggers rum

Mix pineapple, orange, and lime or lemon juices together. Sweeten with the grenadine; then add the rum. Pour into a tall glass with plenty of ice. Jiggle with a barspoon until well frappéed.

PELICAN PECANS

1 10-oz. pkg. pecan halves
2 tbsp. unsalted butter
1½ tsp. ground cumin

¼ tsp. cayenne pepper
2 tbsp. sugar
1 tsp. salt

Preheat the oven to 300°. Place the pecans in a medium-sized bowl. Melt the butter in heavy small saucepan; then stir in the cumin and cayenne for about 15 seconds, or until aromatic. Pour the butter sauce over pecans. Add the sugar and salt and stir to coat. Transfer to a baking pan, and bake until the nuts are toasted, stirring occasionally, for about 20 minutes. Serve warm or at room temperature. Makes about 2½ cups.

EMMES EGGPLANT CAVIER
(Microwave and Conventional)

1 onion, finely chopped
1 green pepper, finely chopped
2 cloves garlic, minced
¼ cup olive oil
1 eggplant (about 1 lb.), peeled and diced
1 6-oz. can tomato paste
¼ cup red wine vinegar

¼ cup chopped pimiento-stuffed green olives or salad olives
2 tsp. sugar
1 tsp. basil
¼ tsp. pepper
½ tsp. salt
cocktail rye, pumpernickel, or crisp crackers

MICROWAVE: Combine the onion, green pepper, garlic, and oil in a 2-quart casserole. Cover tightly with plastic wrap, turning back one edge to vent. Microwave at 100% power for 5 minutes. Stir in the eggplant, tomato paste, vinegar, olives, sugar, basil, pepper, and salt. Cover, leaving a vent, and microwave at 100% power for 10 minutes, stirring once. Stir well, cover, and cook at 70% power for 18 minutes, stirring once. Chill and serve on small slices of bread or crackers. Serves 30.

CONVENTIONAL: Sauté the onion, green pepper, and garlic in the oil in a skillet until the onion is transparent. Add the eggplant, tomato paste, vinegar, olives, sugar, basil, pepper, and salt. Cover and simmer for 1 hour, stirring occasionally. Chill and serve on small slices of bread or crackers. Serves 30.

SO-OO GOO-OOD SALAD

2 16-oz. cans petit pois peas
2 16-oz. cans cut green beans
1 6½-oz. jar chopped
   pimiento
1 large onion, thinly sliced
6 ribs celery, sliced
1 bell pepper, thinly sliced

½ cup vegetable oil
1 cup sugar
1 cup vinegar
1 tbsp. salt
1 tbsp. water
¼ tsp. paprika

Drain the juice from the peas, beans, and pimiento. Mix all the ingredients together in large bowl. Cover and refrigerate for at least 12 hours. Stir the mixture at least twice. Serve chilled. Serves 8.

STOMPIN' SALAD DRESSING

2 tbsp. Creole mustard
2 tbsp. vinegar
¾ cups olive oil or salad oil
¼ tsp. garlic powder

½ tsp. onion powder
¼ tsp. pepper
¼ tsp. horseradish

Place all the ingredients in a blender, and blend until well mixed and thick. Makes about 1 cup.

RIVER RICE SALAD

3 cups cooked rice
4 hard-boiled eggs, chopped
1 cup imitation bacon bits
½ cup chopped pickles
½ cup chopped celery

½ cup chopped onions
½ cup mayonnaise
2 tbsp. Old South French
Dressing (see recipe)

Combine all ingredients. Chill. Serves 12.

OLD SOUTH FRENCH DRESSING

½ cup sugar
¼ cup vinegar
1 tsp. lemon juice
2 tsp. onion salt

⅓ cup catsup
½ cup salad oil
1 tsp. salt
1 tsp. cayenne pepper

Put all the ingredients into a blender and blend well. Pour into a 1½ cup glass or plastic container and refrigerate for at least 24 hours before using. Makes 1½ cups.

CHAI THERE CHOWDER

3 tbsp. butter or margarine
½ cup chopped celery
3 tbsp. flour
½ tsp. salt
¼ tsp. black pepper
4 cups milk

2 cups diced potatoes,
    cooked and peeled
1 16½-oz. can green peas
1 7¾-oz. can salmon, flaked
1 cup shredded cheddar
    cheese

Melt the butter or margarine in a heavy, 3-quart saucepan. Sauté the celery until tender, about 5 minutes. Stir in the flour, salt, and pepper. Remove from heat to gradually stir in the milk; then bring to a boil, stirring constantly. Add the potatoes, peas, and salmon. Reduce heat to low. Simmer for about 5 minutes, then stir in the cheese until it melts. Serves 8.

A GOOD CAJUN GUMBO

2 lb. Kosher smoked
    sausages, cut into ½-inch
    pieces
½ cup vegetable oil
½ cup all-purpose flour
8 stalks celery, chopped
1 bunch parsley, chopped

3 medium onions, chopped
6 cups water
3 tsp. filé
1 tsp. salt
1 tsp. pepper
4 cups hot cooked rice

Brown the sausage slices in a large, heavy skillet or pot. Stir well. Drain on paper towels and set aside.

Combine the oil and flour in the same pot. Cook over medium heat for 15 to 20 minutes, stirring constantly, until mixture (roux) is the color of caramel. Stir in the celery, onions, and parsley. Cook for 5 minutes, stirring occasionally. Add the sausage and water. Bring to a boil; then reduce the heat and simmer, uncovered, for 4 hours. Stir in the filé, salt, and pepper. Serve over hot rice. Serves 12 to 16.

TALLULAH TOMATO SOUP
(Microwave and Conventional)

1 onion, finely chopped
¼ cup pareve margarine
2 tbsp. olive oil
2 lb. ripe tomatoes, coarsely diced
1 10½-oz. can condensed Kosher chicken broth, undiluted

2 tbsp. chopped fresh basil or 1 tsp. dry basil
2 tsp. chopped fresh thyme or ½ tsp. dry thyme
2 tsp. sugar
2 tbsp. cornstarch
3 tbsp. water
salt and pepper to taste

MICROWAVE: Combine the onion, pareve margarine, and oil in a 3-quart glass bowl. Cover tightly with plastic wrap, turning back one edge to vent. Microwave at 100% power for 3 minutes. Stir in the tomatoes, chicken broth, 1 soup can of water, basil, thyme, and sugar. Cover, leaving vent, and microwave at 100% power for 17 minutes, stirring once. Press through a fine sieve. Discard the seeds and skin. Mix the cornstarch and 3 tablespoons of water until smooth; then stir into the soup. Cook at 100% power for 3 to 4 minutes, until the mixture boils. Season with salt and pepper. Serves 4.

CONVENTIONAL: Sauté the onion in the pareve margarine and oil until the onion is transparent. Add the tomatoes, chicken broth, basil, thyme, and sugar. Heat the mixture to boiling; then reduce the heat, cover, and simmer for 30 minutes. Press the mixture through a fine sieve and discard the seeds and skin. Mix the cornstarch with the 3 tablespoons water until smooth, then stir into the soup. Heat to boiling. Boil for 1 minute, season with salt and pepper, and serve. Serves 4.

CAJUN DUCK JAMBALAYA

3 tbsp. vegetable oil
3 tbsp. flour
2 medium onions, chopped
1 cup chopped shallots
2 tbsp. chopped fresh parsley
1 cup chopped celery
1 cup chopped green pepper

2 cloves garlic, minced
2 cups chicken stock
1 cup rice, uncooked
2 tsp. salt
½ tsp. cayenne pepper
4 cups cooked duck meat, cut into bite-sized pieces

In a large, heavy pot, heat the oil. Gradually add the flour, stirring constantly, until the roux is dark brown. Add the onions, shallots, parsley, celery, green pepper, and garlic. Cook until soft. Add the chicken stock, rice, salt, pepper, and duck meat. Bring to a boil, then the lower heat as much as possible. Cook for 1 hour, covered. Stir occasionally. When the rice is done, remove the lid and cook a few more minutes, so the rice will steam dry. Serves 4 to 6.

CHICKEN A LA COKE

1 cup chopped celery
1 cup chopped onion
1 cup catsup
1 tsp. salt
1 tsp. chili powder

1 3-lb. fryer, cut into serving pieces
salt and pepper to taste
flour
2 cups cola

Mix together the chopped celery, onion, catsup, salt, and chili powder. Place in a deep baking dish or a 9x13x2-inch baking pan, spreading the mixture evenly across the bottom of the dish. Sprinkle the chicken pieces with salt and pepper; then dredge in flour. Place the chicken in the dish; then pour the cola over everything. Bake in a preheated oven at 350° for 1½ hours, or until chicken is well done. Turn chicken halfway through the cooking time. Serves 4 to 5.

CREOLE CHICKEN AND SAUCE

¼ cup pareve margarine
2 cups raw chicken breast,
  in 1-inch cubes

fresh parsley
3½ cups Creole Sauce
2 cups cooked rice

Melt the pareve margarine over medium heat in a large pan. Add the chicken cubes and parsley; and sauté for 10 minutes, until the chicken pieces are tender. Stir in the Creole sauce and serve over the rice. Serves 4.

Creole Sauce

2 tbsp. vegetable oil
1 onion, peeled and chopped
2 bell peppers, chopped
3 cups diced tomatoes
3 stalks celery, chopped
2 cups tomato puree
1 tsp. cayenne pepper

2 tbsp. chopped garlic
1 tbsp. chopped parsley
1 cup chicken stock
salt and freshly ground black
  pepper to taste
few drops Tabasco sauce

Heat the vegetable oil in a large saucepan. Add the onion, bell peppers, and tomatoes. Cook, stirring, for one minute; then add the celery. Stir in the tomato puree. Sauté for 5 minutes; then stir in the cayenne pepper, garlic, parsley, chicken stock, salt, pepper, and Tabasco sauce. Reduce the heat, and simmer for 7 minutes. Makes about 3½ cups of sauce.

BIENVILLE'S BEEF WITH IBERVILLE SAUCE

4 beef rib eye steaks
freshly ground pepper to taste
1½ tbsp. olive oil
1 tsp. pareve margarine
¼ cup finely minced shallots

2 tbsp. vinegar
¼ tsp. tarragon
⅓ cup Iberville Sauce (see recipe)

Allow the meat to come to room temperature. Pepper liberally and pat the cracked pepper into the steaks. Heat the oil in a heavy skillet over high heat; then add the steaks. Cook for 3 to 4 minutes; then turn, reduce the heat, and cook until done to desired degree. Remove the steaks and keep them warm.

Pour off the oil. In the same skillet, cook the pareve margarine and shallots for one minute; then add the vinegar and tarragon. Cook until the liquid has nearly evaporated. Remove from the heat, swirl in the Iberville Sauce, bit by bit, until a light sauce is formed. Pour it over the steaks. Serves 4.

IBERVILLE SAUCE

4 tbsp. pareve margarine, softened
¼ tsp. minced garlic

¼ tsp. lemon zest
1 tbsp. minced parsley
½ tsp. lemon juice

Beat all of the ingredients together until well blended. Refrigerate until ready to use. Makes about ⅓ cup.

MACHER'S MOUSSE
(Microwave and Conventional)

2 7-oz. cans tuna, drained
1 small onion, quartered
2 tbsp. lemon juice
¼ tsp. dill

dash pepper
¼ cup mayonnaise
2 egg whites
2 tbsp. chopped parsley

MICROWAVE: Grease a 1-quart fluted glass mold or bowl. Place the tuna, onion, lemon juice, dill, and pepper in a food processor or blender. Process until finely chopped. Place the mixture in a mixing bowl, and stir in the mayonnaise. In a separate bowl, beat the egg whites until soft peaks form. Fold in the tuna mixture and the parsley, then spoon into the prepared mold. Cover tightly with plastic wrap, turning back one edge to vent. Cook at 70% power for 1 minute; then stir the cooked edges to the center. Cover, leaving a vent, and cook 3 minutes more, stirring after 1½ minutes. Let stand, covered, for 5 minutes. Cover the mold with a serving dish, and turn upside down to unmold. Serve warm or chilled. Serves 4 to 6.

CONVENTIONAL: Preheat the oven to 375°. Grease 1-quart fluted mold. Place the tuna, onion, lemon juice, dill, and pepper in a food processor or blender. Process until finely chopped; then place in a mixing bowl and stir in the mayonnaise. Beat the egg whites in a separate bowl until soft peaks form; then fold in the tuna mixture and the parsley. Spoon the mixture into the prepared mold. Set the mold on a rack in a large pan and place in the preheated oven. Add enough boiling water to the pan to come halfway up the side of the mold. Bake for 40 to 50 minutes, or until a knife inserted in the center comes out clean. Cover the mold with a serving dish, and turn upside down to unmold. Serve warm or chilled. Serves 4 to 6.

ACADIAN ASPARAGUS
(Microwave and Conventional)

2 tbsp. grated parmesan
cheese
3 tbsp. butter
¼ cups all-purpose flour
1½ cups milk (1¼ cups for
microwave method)
½ tsp. salt
dash pepper

dash ground nutmeg
½ cup mayonnaise
4 eggs, separated
⅓ cup grated parmesan
cheese
1 10-oz. pkg. frozen asparagus, cooked, drained, and
pureed

CONVENTIONAL: Grease a 1½-quart soufflé dish; then coat it
with the 2 tablespoons of parmesan cheese. Melt the butter in a
saucepan; then stir in the flour. Cook over medium heat, stirring
occasionally, for 3 minutes. Stir in milk and heat to boiling. Boil,
stirring constantly, until thickened. Stir in the salt, pepper, and
nutmeg; then remove from the heat and stir in the mayonnaise. Stir
some of the mayonnaise mixture into the egg yolks; then stir the yolk
mixture into mayonnaise mixture. Fold in the ⅓ cup of cheese and the
asparagus. Beat the egg whites until stiff peaks form; then fold them
into the mixture. Pour the mixture into the prepared soufflé dish.
Bake at 350° until a knife inserted in the side of the puff comes out
clean, 45 to 55 minutes. Serves 5.

MICROWAVE: Grease a 1½-quart microwave-safe soufflé dish.
Coat dish with 2 tablespoons of parmesan cheese. In a 4-cup glass
measure, microwave the butter on high power for 30 seconds, until
melted. Stir in the flour. Microwave on high power for 45 seconds.
Stir in 1½ cups of the milk; then microwave on high for 3 minutes,
stirring every minute, until thick. Stir in the salt, pepper, and nutmeg;
then remove from heat. Stir in the mayonnaise. Stir some of mayonnaise mixture into the egg yolks; then stir the yolk mixture into the
mayonnaise mixture. Fold in ⅓ cup of the cheese and the asparagus.
Beat the egg whites until stiff peaks form; then fold them into the
mixture. Pour the mixture into the prepared soufflé dish. Microwave
at 70% power for 10 minutes, or until set. Rotate the dish ¼ turn
every 2 minutes. Serves 6.

STUFFED KASHERED KRABS

1 egg, beaten
1 cup milk
6 slices toast, cubed
2 tbsp. minced onion
2 tbsp. minced celery
2 tbsp. minced bell pepper
1 clove garlic, minced

2 tbsp. butter
2 cups flaked cooked fish
2 tbsp. finely chopped parsley
salt and pepper to taste
1/4 cup bread crumbs
6 lemon slices, cut thin
paprika

Combine the egg and milk in a bowl. Add the toast and let stand. Sauté the onion, celery, bell pepper, and garlic in the butter. Add the flaked fish, parsley, salt, pepper, and the toast mixture. Mix thoroughly. Place in 6 ramekins or aluminum crab shells, and sprinkle with bread crumbs. Dot with additional butter and place the lemon slices on top. Garnish with paprika. Bake at 350° for 15 minutes, or until browned. Serves 6.

FRUMMEH GRITS FRITTERS

2 8-oz. pkg. uncooked instant
    grits
1 cup water
1/2 cup shredded cheddar
    cheese
1/2 cup shredded Swiss cheese
1 tbsp. chopped chives

1/2 tsp. dried sage leaves
1/2 tsp. dried rosemary leaves
1/8 tsp. ground white pepper
1 egg, beaten
1 tbsp. water
1 cup dry bread crumbs
2 cups vegetable oil

In a 1-quart saucepan, cook the grits in the 1 cup of water according to the package instructions. Cook over low heat until very thick, stirring occasionally. Cool the grits to room temperature; then cover and refrigerate for 2 hours.

Combine the grits, cheeses, chives, sage, rosemary, and pepper. Roll the mixture into scant 1-inch balls. Mix the egg and 1 tablespoon of water. Roll the grits balls in the egg mixture: then in the breadcrumbs.

Heat the oil to 375° in a 2-quart saucepan. Fry the grits balls, 7 or 8 at a time, for 1½ to 3 minutes until they are golden brown. Drain on paper towels; then serve with wooden picks. Makes about 2 dozen.

KINGFISH KARROTS

4 cups cooked carrots
½ tsp. salt
½ tsp. nutmeg
1 egg, beaten
2 tbsp. butter or margarine,
    melted

1 cup dry bread crumbs
vegetable oil for deep frying
parsley sprigs

Mash or press the carrots through a coarse sieve. Add the salt, nutmeg, egg, and butter or margarine; mix thoroughly. Form the mixture into shapes resembling carrots, roll in the bread crumbs; then chill for several hours. Fry in hot oil (380°) until browned. Drain on absorbent paper, tuck a sprig of parsley on top before serving. Serves 8.

FRENCHY'S BREAD

1½ pkg. active dry yeast
1 tbsp. sugar
2 cups warm water (100° to 115°)
1 tbsp. salt

5 to 6 cups all-purpose flour
3 tbsp. yellow cornmeal
1 tbsp. egg white, mixed with 1 tbsp. cold water

Combine the yeast with the sugar and warm water in a large bowl and allow it to proof. Mix the salt with the flour and add them to the yeast mixture, a cup at a time, until you have a stiff dough. Remove the dough to a lightly floured board and knead until it is no longer sticky, about 10 minutes. Add flour as necessary. Place the dough in a greased bowl and turn it to coat the surface. Cover and let rise in a warm place until it is doubled in bulk, 1½ to 2 hours.

Punch down the dough. Place it on a floured board and shape it into two long, French bread-style loaves. Place them on a baking sheet that has been sprinkled with cornmeal but not greased. Slash the tops of the loaves diagonally in two or three places, and brush with the egg wash. Place in a cold oven, set the temperature to 400°, and bake for 35 minutes, until well browned and hollow-sounding when the tops are tapped. Makes 2 loaves.

BOUR-BON BANANAS

2 tbsp. butter
4 tbsp. brown sugar
2 ripe bananas, peeled and sliced lengthwise

⅛ tsp. cinnamon
1 oz. banana liqueur
2 oz. white rum

Melt the butter in a chafing dish. Add the brown sugar and blend well. Add the bananas and sauté. Sprinkle with cinnamon; then pour the banana liqueur and rum over the bananas. Ignite the liquid, basting the bananas with the flaming liquid. Serve when the flame dies out. Serves 2 to 3.

LOUISIANA PARISH PIE

3 cups cooked red beans
1 13-oz. can evaporated milk
2 eggs, beaten
1 cup sugar
½ tsp. salt

1 tsp. cinnamon
½ tsp. cloves
½ tsp. nutmeg
2 unbaked 9-inch pie shells

Preheat the oven to 375°. Mash enough of the cooked beans to make 2 cups, and place in a blender, a portion at a time, with the evaporated milk. Blend until smooth. Combine with the eggs, sugar, salt, and spices. Pour into the unbaked pie shells. Bake for 1 hour, or until a knife inserted into center comes out clean. Makes two 9-inch pies.

TANTE POLLY'S PRALINES

1 cup brown sugar
1 cup white sugar
½ cup cream

2 tbsp. butter
1 cup pecan meats

Dissolve the sugars in the cream and bring them to a boil, stirring occasionally. Add the butter and pecans and cook until the syrup reaches the soft ball stage (238°). Cool without disturbing; then beat until somewhat thickened, but not until it loses its gloss. Drop by tablespoon onto a well-greased flat surface or on a waxed paper-lined surface. The candy will flatten out into large cakes. Makes about 20 pralines.

TEXAS
The Lone Star State

At a time when twelve British colonies were struggling on the East Coast, a southwestern territory known as Texas was just beginning to develop.

In the early 1500s, Spain sent explorers to Texas country, seeking "glory, God, and gold." Instead, they found Pueblo Indians living in adobe *haciendas* near what is now El Paso. The word Texas comes from the Indian word *Tejas,* meaning "friends or allies," and Texans proudly claim it means the same today.

The early Spanish conquistadors, in shining armor complete with plumed hats, undaunted by their fruitless search for riches, continued to explore Texas. Except for five years of French rule in the late 1600s, it was Spanish settlers and culture that dominated the territory for the first one hundred years. Missionaries who worked among the Indians established mission schools throughout the territory. These schools became the first outposts of civilization.

Of all the states in the union, Texas is the only one that was once a nation in its own right. In 1836, after the famed siege of the Alamo in San Antonio, Texans won their independence from Mexico and formed an independent republic.

The young republic was without money and was continually threatened by raiding Indians and Mexicans. During this period of Texas history, the flavor that is unique to Texas took root. Tough rawhide cowboys, fast stagecoaches, and gunmen quick on the draw left their indelible mark on Texas. Law and order were nonexistent. The new republic had become part of the Wild West. Because of the constant threats of hostility and lawlessness, concerned citizens took matters in their own hands and formed what is known today as the Texas Rangers. Expert horsemen and marksmen, the Rangers were instrumental in taming the territory, but they did little to tame the budget.

The republic was faced with a growing debt. As the debt grew, Texans began to believe that their future would be more secure as part of the United States. While the South was eager to admit Texas as a state, the North objected to admitting another slave state to the Union. After a bitter fight over the slavery issue, Texas was formally admitted to the Union in 1845 as the 28th state.

With the country at odds and war clouds gathering, the outburst of the Civil War became inevitable. Texas raised the Stars and Bars to become the seventh state to join the Confederacy, formally seceding from the Union on February 1, 1861. However, Texas fared no better in the war than the rest of the Confederacy. Union forces invaded Texas, capturing Galveston and moving on through the territory. It was at Palmito Hill, near Brownsville, that the last Civil War battle was fought in 1865.

As with the other southern states, the war came at a terrible cost. Texas suffered its share of physical destruction and economic collapse. However, unlike most of the other southern states, Texas' climb back from bitter defeat was quite swift. With the rest of the nation in need of beef, Texans returning from the war discovered that their fortunes could be made by breeding longhorn cattle and driving them north to railroad centers. Historic and picturesque cattle trails stretched from San Antonio to Dodge City. Rich soil supported a bounty of agriculture and brought additional resources to the state. The resulting growth and prosperity were remarkable; by 1870, Texas was readmitted to the Union.

Texas began to boom in the twentieth century with the discovery of oil fields. "Black gold" was the cry from border to border. Oil refineries, factories, and mills sprang up, and ports opened to foreign trade. There was no end to the glorious heights to which Texas rose. Today, Texas looks up to outer space.

In retrospect, six flags have flown over Texas: Spanish, French, Mexican, Republic of Texas (a flag with a single star, thus the sobriquet of the "Lone Star State"), the Confederate Stars and Bars, and the American flag. All of them have influenced Texas in one way or another.

It is no surprise that these cultural influences have filtered down to the food Texans eat. Tex-Mex cooking is a specialty. Most Texans are raised on Mexican food. To Texans, barbeque is more of a religion than a means of cooking food. Ask a group of Texans where to find the best barbeque, and sparks fly—all claim theirs to be the best. By the time you have gone from east to west and north to south in the vast Lone Star State, you too will have tasted your favorite recipe. You'll enjoy it all-the-more under the stars at night, which are big and bright, "deep in the heart of Texas."

TO PRESERVE BEEF

Hang up the beef for 3 or 4 days, till it becomes tender. Rub it down with a mixture of bay salt, brown sugar, saltpetre, pepper, and allspice. Now wrap the meat tightly in a cloth and hang in a warm place for about 2 weeks. If you desire a smokey flavor, hang for some time in a chimney corner.

CON QUESO DIP
(Microwave)

2 8-oz. pkg. cream cheese, softened
½ cup salsa

1 chopped shallot, with top
tortilla chips

Mix the cream cheese, salsa, and chopped shallot until well blended. Spread the cheese mixture in a microwaveable pie plate or bowl. Microwave on high for 3 to 4 minutes, or until thoroughly heated, stirring every 2 minutes. Serve with tortilla chips. Makes 2 cups.

GOTTENYU! GUACAMOLE

1 medium onion, chopped
2 medium tomatoes, chopped
1 clove garlic, minced
2 tsp. salt

2 avocados
2 tbsp. lemon juice
1 to 2 tsp. hot pepper sauce

Combine the chopped onion and tomatoes. Blend in the garlic and salt. Pare the avocados and mash the meat, blending it with the lemon juice. Combine the avocado with the tomato-onion mixture and season to taste with the pepper sauce. Serves 4 to 6.

MOSHE'S MEXICAN SALAD

4 12-oz. cans shoe peg corn (white), drained
¼ cup chopped red bell pepper
½ cup chopped green onion
2 tbsp. chopped jalapeno peppers
½ cup mayonnaise

Mix all the ingredients together in a large bowl. Chill before serving. Serves 12 to 16.

COWBOY CORN SOUP

2 cups corn, canned or fresh
1 cup boiling water
1 tbsp. grated onion
2 tbsp. pareve margarine
2 tbsp. flour
3 cups beef stock
1 tbsp. salsa
hot pepper sauce to taste

Grate or finely chop the corn into a saucepan, add the boiling water and onion, and cook for 15 minutes. Strain. Melt the pareve margarine in a deep skillet and stir in flour. Add the stock and seasonings; then cook, stirring constantly, for 5 minutes. Stir in the strained corn pulp, and cook for 10 minutes over medium heat. Serves 4 to 6.

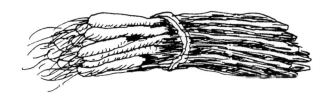

ZAPATA ZUP

1 lb. beef chuck or brisket
1 tbsp. cornstarch
3 tbsp. chili powder
2 tsp. ground cumin
4 tbsp. olive oil
1 large onion, peeled and chopped
3 cloves garlic, peeled and minced

1 16-oz. can tomatoes
1 4-oz. can chopped green chiles
1 8-oz. can whole kernel corn
1 qt. Kosher beef broth
½ cup Kosher red wine
¼ cup wine vinegar
salt and pepper to taste

Slice beef diagonally into ¼-inch thick strips. Combine the cornstarch, chili powder, and cumin. In a bowl, toss the meat strips in 1 tablespoon of the oil. Add the cornstarch mixture and toss to coat. Reserve any cornstarch mixture left in bowl.

In large pan or dutch oven, stir fry the beef strips in 1 tablespoon of the oil until the beef is cooked as desired. Remove the beef strips from the pan and set aside. Cook the onion in the remaining 2 tablespoons of oil until the onion is soft. Add the garlic and sauté until it is soft, about 2 minutes. Add the tomatoes and their liquid, green chiles with liquid, corn with liquid, beef broth, wine, and wine vinegar. Add the remaining cornstarch mixture to the soup; then bring it to a boil and simmer for about 20 minutes, adding water if the mixture becomes too thick. Add the beef strips and simmer for an additional 5 minutes. Season to taste with salt and pepper. Serves 4 to 6.

BIG D BARBECUE SAUCE

1 15-oz. can tomato sauce
¼ cup wine vinegar
¼ cup chili sauce
¼ cup firmly packed brown
  sugar
2 tbsp. Worcestershire sauce

3 tbsp. grated onion
1 tsp. paprika
1 tsp. dijon mustard
½ tsp. chili powder
⅛ tsp. hot pepper sauce (optional)

Combine all the ingredients in a saucepan. Bring to a boil; then reduce the heat and simmer for 15 minutes. Makes about 2½ cups of sauce.

SALSA FOR THE SHERIFF

1 28-oz. can whole tomatoes,
  drained
4 shallots with tops, finely
  chopped
1 4-oz. can mild chopped
  green chiles, drained
¼ cup finely chopped green
  pepper

1 tbsp. Worcestershire sauce
1¼ tsp. sugar
¾ tsp. garlic salt
⅛ tsp. oregano leaves
corn chips or tortilla chips

Remove seeds from the tomatoes and chop. Combine them with the remaining ingredients and chill. Serve with corn or tortilla chips. Makes 2 cups of sauce.

HASE JALAPENO SAUCE

2 tbsp. finely chopped canned
  jalapeno chiles
1½ tsp. liquid drained from
  canned jalapenos

1½ tsp. finely chopped onion
1½ tsp. finely chopped
  tomato

Combine jalapenos, jalapeno liquid, onion, and tomato. Mix well. Serve as a sauce with tacos. Makes about ¼ cup.

DAPPER SNAPPER

2 lb. red snapper fillets
1 tsp. salt
2 tbsp. melted butter
1 cup chopped onion
2 tbsp. olive oil
⅔ cup (6-oz. can) tomato
  paste

1⅔ cups (14½-oz. can) solid
  pack tomatoes
1 tbsp. chopped hot green
  chiles
1 tbsp. capers
⅓ cup stuffed olives
1 tsp. salt
⅛ tsp. pepper

Place the snapper fillets in a shallow, buttered 2-quart baking dish. Sprinkle with salt; then brush them with melted butter. Bake the snapper in the oven at 350° until the fish flakes easily with a fork, or about 30 to 40 minutes.

In a saucepan, sauté the onion in the oil until tender. Add the tomato paste, tomatoes, chilies, capers, olives, salt, and pepper. Simmer over medium heat for 20 minutes. Serve the sauce over the baked red snapper. Garnish with additional olives and watercress if desired. Serves 6.

KIBBITZER KRAB TACOS

2 tbsp. vegetable oil
1 medium onion, thinly sliced
1 medium green pepper, cut
 in thin strips
1 lb. Kosher imitation crabmeat
⅓ cup half-and-half or
 whipping cream

¼ cup freshly chopped
 cilantro
salt and pepper to taste
8 taco shells, warmed
1 cup grated Kosher cheddar
 cheese

Heat the oil in a large pan over medium-high heat. When it is hot, sauté the onions until they are translucent, about 4 minutes. Add the green pepper strips and imitation crabmeat; then sauté for about 1 minute more.

Reduce the heat to medium; then add the cream and cilantro. Blend well. Cook for about 2 minutes until the sauce is slightly thickened. Season with salt and pepper.

Divide the filling among the eight taco shells, topping each with grated cheese. Serves 8.

BBQ'D BEHAYMA

1 3- to 3½-pound boneless
 beef brisket, trimmed
1 large onion, sliced
2 cloves garlic, minced

1 bay leaf
½ cup beer
1 18-oz. bottle barbecue
 sauce

Place the meat, fat side up, in a shallow baking pan. Place the onions, garlic, and bay leaf on top of the meat; then pour the beer over the meat. Cover and bake at 300° for 2 hours. Remove the meat from the pan and drain the liquid, reserving ½ cup. Return the meat and the reserved liquid to the pan. Pour the barbecue sauce over the meat; then continue baking, uncovered, for 1 hour or until the meat is tender. Serves 4 to 6.

MEXICALI CHICKEN

3- to 3½-pound cut-up frying chicken
¼ cup flour
1 tsp. seasoned salt
⅛ tsp. pepper
¼ cup pareve margarine
1 cup chopped onion
2½ cups canned solid pack tomatoes
1½ cups whole kernel corn, drained
¼ cup chopped green chiles, seeded
½ cup sliced ripe olives
2 small cloves garlic, crushed
3 tbsp. vinegar
1 tbsp. chili powder
1 tsp. tarragon

Coat the chicken pieces with a mixture of the flour, salt, and pepper. Melt the pareve margarine in a frying pan. Add the chicken and cook until it is golden brown. Remove from pan, drain, and arrange in a 3-quart casserole.

Sauté the onion in the drippings from the chicken. Add the tomatoes, corn, chiles, olives, garlic, vinegar, chili powder, and tarragon. Heat the mixture to boiling; then pour it over the chicken. Cover and bake at 350° for about one hour until the chicken is tender. Serves 4 to 6.

TATA'S TURKEY
(Microwave)

1 lb. raw ground turkey
1 medium onion, coarsely chopped
1 clove garlic, minced
1½ tsp. chili powder
½ tsp. salt
1 medium zucchini squash, cut into ½-inch chunks
1 medium green pepper, cut into ½-inch chunks
1 8-oz. can tomato sauce
1 15- to 19-oz. can black, white, or red beans
1 tbsp. chopped parsley

In a 2½-quart casserole, microwave the ground turkey, onion, garlic, chili powder, and salt; covered, on high for 3 to 5 minutes until turkey is no longer pink. Stir to break up the turkey. Add the zucchini squash, green pepper, and tomato sauce. Cook, covered, for 9 to 11 minutes until the vegetables are tender, stirring occasionally.

Add the beans with their liquid; then cook, covered, for 3 to 4 minutes, or until hot. Sprinkle with 1 tablespoon of chopped parsley. Serves 6.

TEXAS TUNA TOMATOES

6 large firm tomatoes
1 green pepper, diced
1 small hot chile, seeded and minced
1 onion, diced
2 tbsp. vegetable oil
½ tsp. chili powder
½ cup cooked rice
½ cup Kosher bread crumbs
1 9½-oz. tuna, drained
salt to taste
¾ cup shredded Kosher cheddar cheese

Cut the tops from the tomatoes. Scoop out and discard the seeds and pulp. Brown the green pepper, chile, and onion in oil over medium heat. Add the chili powder, rice, bread crumbs, and drained tuna. Mix and simmer for 2 minutes. Season with salt; then fill the tomato shells with the mixture. Place in a greased baking dish, and top with cheese. Bake at 375° for 30 minutes. Serves 6.

BONDITT BURRITOS

1 cup mild green taco sauce
8 6-inch corn tortillas
¾ lb. lean, boneless steak
vegetable cooking spray

1 cup julienne-cut 3x¼-inch
green bell pepper
1 medium onion, cut in ¼-
inch wedges

Brush 1 tablespoon of taco sauce on both sides of each tortilla. Set aside. Trim the fat from the steak; then slice it diagonally across the grain into thin strips. Set aside.

Coat a large, nonstick skillet with vegetable cooking spray. Place it over medium-high heat until it is hot. Add the bell pepper and onion wedges; sauté 3 minutes. Add the steak; then cook for 2 minutes or until desired degree of doneness.

Spoon ½ cup of the mixture onto each tortilla; then roll them up, and place them, seam side down, on a broiler rack. Top with the remaining ½ cup of taco sauce.

Place the rack on a broiler pan and broil, 4 inches from the heat, for 5 minutes or until browned. Serves 4.

CONQUISTADOR CHILI

2 lb. lean ground beef
2 medium onions, chopped
1 medium green pepper,
seeded and chopped
1 stalk celery, chopped
1 clove garlic, minced
2 16-oz. cans tomatoes,
chopped
1 15-oz. can tomato sauce
1½ cups water

½ cup pickled jalapeno peppers, rinsed and chopped
¼ cup chili powder
1 tbsp. ground red pepper
½ tsp. salt
½ tsp. black pepper
1 bay leaf
1 15½-oz. can red kidney
beans, drained

In a large saucepan or dutch oven, cook the ground beef, onions, green pepper, celery, and garlic until the meat is browned and the vegetables are tender. Do not drain.

Stir in the undrained tomatoes, tomato sauce, water, rinsed and chopped jalapeno peppers, chili powder, ground red pepper, salt, black pepper, and bay leaf. Bring the mixture to boiling; then reduce the heat. Simmer, uncovered, for 1½ hours, stirring occasionally. Stir in the beans; then cook for 30 minutes. Remove the bay leaf before serving. Serves 8 to 10.

KALLEH TAMALE PIE

½ cup chopped green pepper
1 clove garlic, minced
1 cup minced onion
1 tbsp. vegetable oil
1 lb. ground beef
1 tbsp. flour
½ cup chopped pitted ripe olives
2½ cups solid pack tomatoes
2 tbsp. chili powder
⅛ tsp. red pepper sauce
1 tsp. salt
⅛ tsp. pepper
1½ cups (12-oz. can) whole kernel corn, drained
3 cups water
1 cup cornmeal
½ tsp. salt
½ cup Kosher seasoned bread crumbs

In large frying pan, sauté the green pepper, garlic, and onion in the oil. Add the beef and continue cooking until the meat is brown, stirring occasionally. Drain the excess fat; then blend in the flour. Add the ripe olives, tomatoes, chili powder, red pepper sauce, salt, and pepper. Simmer for 15 minutes over low heat; then add the corn and mix well.

Heat 2 cups of the water to boiling. Mix the cornmeal with the ½ teaspoon of salt and the remaining 1 cup of cold water. Pour the mixture into the boiling water, stirring constantly. Cook until thickened over medium heat, about 15 to 20 minutes.

Line the bottom and sides of greased 13x9x2-inch baking dish with the cooked cornmeal. Fill the pie with the meat and tomato mixture; then sprinkle the top with bread crumbs. Bake at 350° for 30 minutes. Serves 6.

GREEN BEANS POR GALVESTON

1 clove garlic, minced
¼ cup chopped green pepper
1 cup onion rings
1 tbsp. vegetable oil
1 14½-oz. can can solid pack
  tomatoes

¼ cup chopped green chiles
1 tsp. salt
⅛ tsp. pepper
⅛ tsp. oregano leaves
2 9-oz. pkg. frozen cut or
  whole green beans

In large frying pan, sauté the garlic, green pepper, and onion rings until tender in the 1 tablespoon of vegetable oil. Add the tomatoes, green chiles, salt, pepper, and oregano leaves. Mix well to break the tomatoes. Bring to a boil; then reduce the heat and simmer for 15 minutes.

Cook the two 9-ounce packages of frozen green beans according to the package directions. Drain them and place in center of a vegetable bowl. Spoon the tomato mixture over the beans and serve at once. Serves 4 to 6.

LONE STAR SUCCOTASH

¼ lb. Beef Frye (about 8
  slices), diced
1 large onion, chopped
1 10-oz. can tomatoes and
  green chiles
2 tsp. chili powder
¼ tsp. hot pepper sauce

1 17-oz. can whole kernel
  corn, drained
1 15-oz. can pinto beans,
  drained
1 10-oz. pkg. frozen lima
  beans, thawed
⅓ cup sliced pimiento

In a large skillet, cook the Beef Frye until browned; then remove it and set aside. Drain the Beef Frye fat; then, in the same skillet, sauté the onion until tender, about 3 minutes. Stir in the tomatoes, chili powder, and pepper sauce. Return the cooked Beef Frye to the skillet; then simmer for 5 minutes. Add the corn, pinto beans, lima beans, and pimiento; heat through. Serves 6.

TAKA TACOS

12 taco shells
3 cups Chicken Filling
shredded pareve cheese

chopped onion and tomato
shredded lettuce
picante sauce

Heat the taco shells on a cookie sheet in a 350° oven for 5 to 7 minutes. Fill each shell with ¼ cup of chicken filling. Garnish with pareve cheese, onion, tomato, and lettuce. Top with picante sauce. Serves 4 to 6.

Chicken Filling

3 cups shredded or finely chopped cooked chicken
¾ cup picante sauce
⅓ cup green onion slices

1 tsp. ground cumin
½ tsp. oregano leaves, crushed

Combine all the ingredients in a saucepan; then simmer for 5 minutes, stirring occasionally. Serve as a filling for tacos, tostadas, or burritos. Makes about three cups.

RIO GRANDE RICE

1 tbsp. vegetable oil
1 tsp. chili powder
½ tsp. garlic salt
1 cup regular rice, cooked

1 12-oz. can Mexicorn, drained
1 4-oz. can chopped green chiles, drained

In a skillet, heat the oil, chili powder, and garlic salt on high. Stir thoroughly. Reduce the heat to medium-high; then add the rice and sauté for about 2 minutes. Stir in the Mexicorn and chopped green chiles. Cook until heated through, about 5 minutes. Serves 4.

LOS ZOLLY'S ZUCCHINI

4 to 5 large zucchini
2 tbsp. butter or margarine
2 cloves garlic, crushed
¼ cup minced onion
2 tomatillos, chopped
3 tbsp. diced pimiento
2 egg yolks

1 cup crushed corn chips
1 cup shredded Kosher colby
  cheese
1 8-oz. can tomato sauce
2 tbsp. diced green chiles
corn chips

Place the whole zucchini in a large skillet with 1 inch of boiling salted water. Cover and cook for about 7 minutes. Drain and rinse them quickly in cold water to stop cooking. Cut off the top portions lengthwise, and scoop out the pulp to leave a ½-inch-thick shell. Dice the pulp.

Melt the butter or margarine in a small skillet. Sauté the garlic and onion for about 1 minute; then add the tomatillos and cook until tender. Add the pimiento and diced zucchini pulp. Reduce the heat and simmer for about 10 minutes. Stir a small amount of the mixture into the egg yolks; then mix it into the pan. Add the crushed corn chips and half of the cheese. Place the shells in lightly greased, shallow baking pan. Fill each shell with stuffing and bake at 350° for 20 minutes.

Combine the tomato sauce and chiles, heat, then pour over the zucchini. Sprinkle with remaining cheese and bake for 5 more minutes. Garnish with whole corn chips. Serves 4 to 6.

REBBE'S REFRIED BEANS

1 lb. dry pinto beans	1 tbsp. salt
8 cups water	2 cloves garlic, minced
⅔ cup picante sauce	¼ cup pareve margarine
¼ cup finely chopped onion	salt to taste

Sort through the beans, discarding any foreign material; then thoroughly wash and drain them. Combine the beans, water, ⅓ cup of the picante sauce, onion, salt, and garlic in a dutch oven. Bring the mixture to a boil; then reduce the heat and cover. Simmer for 3 to 4 hours, until the beans are tender and may be mashed easily. Add water as needed, and stir occasionally.

Drain the beans, reserving the liquid. Return the beans to the dutch oven or transfer them to the large bowl of an electric mixer. Add the pareve margarine and the remaining ⅓ cup of picante sauce. Beat on low speed with the electric mixer until the beans are as smooth as you prefer. Add the reserved cooking liquid, a small amount at a time, until the desired consistency is achieved. Add salt to taste; then fry them in a skillet until the beans are well heated. Serves 8.

SANTA CHANA SQUASH

4 to 5 medium-sized yellow squash	2 tbsp. butter
1 large onion, minced	salt to taste
½ cup celery, minced	1 to 2 tsp. hot pepper sauce
¼ cup bell pepper, minced	½ cup bread crumbs
	1 to 2 tbsp. butter

Peel and cube the squash. Place the squash and the chopped vegetables in a small amount of water in a skillet, and simmer until tender and all the liquid is gone. Add the 2 tablespoons of butter, salt, and pepper sauce. Put the mixture in a greased, 2-quart casserole. Cover with bread crumbs and dot with remaining butter. Bake at 350° until the crumbs have browned. Serves 6.

TEX-MEX SHABBOS CHOLENT

1 lb. dry pinto beans
1 qt. water
2 lb. lean beef, cubed
2 tbsp. vegetable oil
1 8-oz. can tomato sauce
4 cloves garlic, minced
2 small onions, chopped
1 chile pepper, chopped

1 tbsp. flour
1 tbsp. chili powder
1 tbsp. cumin
1 tbsp. vinegar
1½ tsp. salt
pinch thyme
1 tsp. chopped fresh cilantro

Cook the beans in the water for 2 hours. Brown the beef in the oil; then combine the beans, their liquid, meat, and the remaining ingredients in a dutch oven and cover tightly. Place in a 250° oven and bake for 24 hours. Serve with tortilla chips. Serves 6.

ARROZ PUDDING

2 cups cooked rice, cold
1 tbsp. cocoa
2 tbsp. sugar
¼ tsp. salt

1 cup shredded coconut
1 tsp. vanilla extract
2 egg whites
2 tbsp. sugar

Combine the rice, cocoa, sugar, salt, coconut, and vanilla. Place the mixture in a greased baking dish. Beat the egg whites until frothy, add 2 tablespoons of sugar, and continue beating until stiff and the peaks hold. Cover the rice mixture with the meringue, and brown in a 300° oven. Serves 8.

TEX-MEX-JEWISH CHEESECAKE

12 graham crackers
2 lb. cream cheese
1¾ cups sugar
3 tbsp. flour
¼ tsp. salt
grated rind of 1 lemon

grated rind of ½ orange
5 eggs
2 egg yolks
2 tbsp. papaya juice
1 cup heavy cream, divided

Preheat the oven to 475°. Dampen the graham crackers; then crush them to use as a crust in a medium-sized cake pan. Beat the cheese; then mix in the sugar, flour, and salt. Keep the mixture smooth. Add the rinds, eggs, egg yolks, papaya juice, and ¼ cup of the cream. Turn the mixture into the crust. Bake for 15 minutes. Reduce the heat to 200°; then bake 1 hour more. Let stand for 15 minutes to cool. Whip remaining cream to top cake. Serves 10.

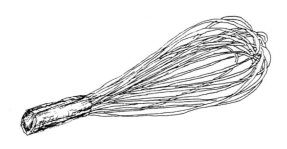

VIRGINIA
The Old Dominion State

Jamestown, Williamsburg, Yorktown, Richmond, Appomattox, Bull Run, Manassas. George Washington, Thomas Jefferson, Robert E. Lee, Stonewall Jackson. This is Virginia, the Old Dominion State. No state has played a more important role in American history. It has withstood injustices and adversity, survived geographic and human destruction, and has become a symbol of all that has made this country great.

Virginia, named for "the Virgin Queen", Elizabeth I of England, is known as the Old Dominion. Charles II of England placed the Arms of Virginia on the royal shield, giving Virginia equal status with England, Scotland, and Ireland—the other dominions.

Thirteen years before the pilgrims landed at Plymouth Rock, 104 English men and boys settled a site on the banks of the James River in Virginia. Thus, in 1607, Jamestown, the first permanent colony in the New World, was established. At the time of the settlement of Jamestown, the Powhatan Indians were unfriendly to the "white man" settlers. When John Rolfe, best known for his successful tobacco crop, married Pocahontas, the daughter of Chief Powhatan, the struggling colony enjoyed several years of peace with the Indians.

Throughout the 1600s, Indian massacres, armed rebellions, and uprisings against British tyranny kept Virginia in a constant state of upheaval. By the turn of the century, however, Virginia had progressed and prospered. Slaves worked the large estates, the tobacco industry was flourishing, and population was on the rise. The first free school had been established in Hampton; and William and Mary, the second oldest colonial college, was chartered.

As the years passed, the prosperity in Virginia led to ever-increasing taxes and social unrest. Because the House of Burgesses protested the tax increases, the governor ordered the House dissolved. In 1775 in St. John's Church in Richmond, Patrick Henry delivered his famous "Give Me Liberty or Give Me Death" speech—sentiments that echoed throughout the colony. Under the leadership of Patrick Henry, Richard Henry Lee, and Thomas Jefferson, Virginia patriots organized their opposition to Great Britain. The American Revolution became imminent and, in 1776, the Declaration of Independence, written by Jefferson, was adopted by the Continental Congress.

The colonists declared their independence; then they had to win it.

The conflict began with George Washington placed, by the second Continental Congress, in charge of all colonial troops. On the battlefront, General Washington led his army through long and harsh battles. Many stories have been told of the inhumane conditions and sufferings endured by the soldiers. In the end, however, they emerged victorious.

America's colonial days began and ended in Virginia, a mere 25 miles apart. On the battlefields of Yorktown in 1781, the United States won its independence from England when British General Charles Cornwallis surrendered to George Washington. Soon thereafter, a new government was firmly established and a governing body was needed. Because of his great leadership, George Washington was elected as the first president of the United States.

For decades, Virginia's statesmen were leaders in shaping the policy of the new nation. However, internal issues were soon to split the people of Virginia. The disputes between eastern and western Virginia were increased by the question that split the union—the issue of slavery. In 1859, John Brown's raid on Harper's Ferry spurred on the Civil War. Virginia became the eighth state to secede from the Union in 1861; and Richmond became the new capital of the Confederacy.

Walt Whitman, the poet, described the Civil War very simply as "a strange, sad war." Virginians felt the drama and sweep of the Civil War for four long, tragic years. It began at Bull Run and ended at Appomattox with General Robert E. Lee's surrender to General Ulysses S. Grant on April 9, 1865. In between were thousands of battles, skirmishes, and engagements that left Virginia scarred and defenseless—and deeply aware of the struggle that lay ahead to rebuild the war-torn land.

Following the Civil War, dishonest politicians from the North descended upon the stricken South and rendered the populace helpless. Virginia went through difficult periods of readjustment. Through their climb back, Virginians held on to many of their traditions—particularly with the home. Even today, they continue the time-honored tradition of setting tables with a variety of dishes: Indian corn muffins, spoon bread, country chicken, and chowder. From the golden age of Virginia to the present, game, wildlife, and seafood were and still are in abundance; and each meal is looked upon as a lavish treat.

A visit to the myriad of historical sites, together with leisurely dining in colorful taverns, will surely culminate with a plea to "Carry me back to Old Virgini."

SALLY LUNN

Beat four Eggs well; then melt a large Tablespoonful of Butter. Put it in a Teacup of warm Water, and put it to the Eggs with a Teaspoon of Salt and a Teacup of Yeast (this means Potato Yeast); beat in a Quart of Flour making the Batter stiff enough for a Spoon to stand in. Put it to rise before the Fire the Night before. Beat it over in the Morning, grease your Cake mould and put it in Time enough to rise before baking. Should you want it for Supper, make it up at ten o'Clock in the Morning in the Winter and twelve o'Clock in the Summer.

VEL-KUMM VASSAIL

1 cup sugar	2 cups orange juice
4 cinnamon sticks	6 cups dry red wine
3 lemon slices	½ cup lemon juice
½ cup water	1 cup dry sherry
2 cups pineapple juice	2 lemons, sliced

Boil the sugar, cinnamon sticks, and 3 lemon slices in the water for 5 minutes; then strain. Discard the cinnamon sticks and lemon slices.

Combine and heat, but do not boil, the remaining ingredients. Combine them with the syrup, garnish with the lemon slices, and serve hot. Serves 20.

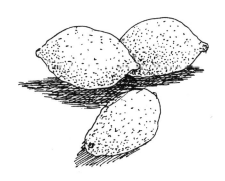

LEFFEL SPOON BREAD

1½ cups water
2 cups milk
1½ cups cornmeal
1¼ tsp. salt

1½ tsp. sugar
2 tbsp. butter
5 eggs
1 tbsp. baking powder

Preheat the oven to 350°. Grease a large, shallow baking dish. Combine the water and milk in a saucepan, and heat to simmer. Add the cornmeal, salt, sugar, and butter; then stir over medium heat until the mixture is thickened, about 5 minutes. Remove from the heat.

Beat the eggs with the baking powder until they are very light and fluffy. Add them to the cornmeal mixture. Mix well. Pour into prepared dish and bake at 350° for 45 to 50 minutes. Serve hot. Serves 8.

VIRGINIA SALLY LUNN

1 pkg. yeast
¼ cup warm water
2 cups scalded milk
⅔ cup vegetable shortening

2 tsp. salt
¼ cup sugar
3 eggs, beaten
6 cups flour

Sprinkle the yeast over the water, then stir to dissolve. Combine the milk, shortening, salt, and sugar in a mixing bowl, and allow to cool to lukewarm. Add the yeast and eggs, and beat until smooth. Add the flour gradually, beating well after each addition. Let rise until doubled in bulk, then punch it down. Place in a large, greased pan and let rise until doubled in bulk. Bake at 350° for about 1 hour. Makes 1 loaf.

MIL'S AND SYL'S DILLS

4 lb. cucumbers
7 tbsp. dill seed
14 cloves garlic
49 peppercorns

3 cups white vinegar
1 cup salt
3 qt. water

Wash the cucumbers and allow them to stand in cold water for 8 hours, or overnight. Drain the cucumbers and place them carefully in pint jars. Add 1 tablespoon dill, 2 cloves garlic, and 7 peppercorns to each jar.

Combine the vinegar, salt, and water in a kettle; then bring to a complete boil. Fill the jars with the vinegar mixture, making sure that cucumbers are completely covered, but leaving ¼ inch of space at the top of the jars. Process in a water-bath canner for 15 minutes. Complete seals, if necessary, after removing jars from canner. Yields 7 pints.

DOMINION DANDELION SALAD

1 lb. young, tender
  dandelion greens
4 thick slices Beef Frye
½ cup salad dressing of your
  choice
1 egg, lightly beaten

1 tsp. salt
1 tbsp. flour
2 tbsp. sugar
¼ cup vinegar
¼ cup water
2 hard-cooked eggs, sliced

Wash the dandelion greens, roll them in a cloth, and pat them dry. Place them in a salad bowl. Fry the Beef Frye until crisp; then drain, pouring the drippings over the dandelion greens.

Blend the salad dressing, egg, salt, flour, sugar, vinegar, and water together; then pour the mixture into the skillet. Bring to a boil and cook, stirring constantly, until thickened. While hot, pour it over the dandelion greens and toss well. Crumble the Beef Frye over the greens and toss lightly. Garnish with the egg slices and serve immediately. Serves 6.

FARPOTSHKET SOUP
(Microwave)

2 medium carrots, thinly sliced

1 large potato, peeled and cut into ½-inch cubes

1 medium onion, sliced

1 cup sliced celery

1½ cups hot water

1½ cups cooked cubed stew beef

2 tbsp. flour

1 8-oz. can tomato sauce

2 tsp. instant Kosher beef soup mix

½ tsp. salt

¼ tsp. basil

⅛ tsp. pepper

1 cup frozen peas

In a 3-quart casserole, combine the carrots, potato, onion, celery, and water. Cover. Microwave on high for 8 to 10 minutes, until vegetables are tender. Stir after half of the cooking time has passed.

In a small bowl, toss the beef cubes with the flour to coat them. Combine the beef with the tomato sauce, beef soup mix, seasonings, peas and cooked vegetables. Cover. Microwave on high for 7 to 9 minutes, or until thoroughly heated. Serves 6.

SHEPZEL'S SPLIT PEA SOUP

1 16-oz pkg. dry split peas

1 lb. soup meat

3 qt. water

1 cup finely chopped celery

1 cup finely chopped onions

2 carrots, chopped (optional)

2 tbsp. lemon pepper seasoning

3 tsp. salt

1 tsp. Worcestershire sauce

1 lemon, thinly sliced

parsley

Put all the ingredients, except the lemon slices and parsley, in a large pot. Bring the mixture to a boil; then reduce the heat. Simmer for about 2 hours, or until the meat is fork-tender and the peas can be easily mashed. Remove the meat, chop it into small pieces, and return it to the pot. Cook for an additional 15 minutes. Pour into soup bowls, garnish with lemon slices, and sprinkle with parsley. Serves 8 to 10.

FOUNDING FATHERS FLOUNDER

2 lb. fresh flounder fillets
salt and pepper
2 tbsp. lemon juice
¼ lb. Kosher saltine crackers
¾ cup almonds, sliced

1 egg, beaten
¼ cup milk
1 cup all-purpose flour
½ cup vegetable oil
½ cup butter

Divide the flounder into 6 portions and season them with salt, pepper, and lemon juice. Coarsely crumble the crackers and mix them with the almonds. Beat the egg and milk together. Dredge the flounder in the flour, dip into the egg-milk mixture; then roll it in the cracker-almond mixture, patting down firmly so the mixture adheres.

Heat the oil and butter in a heavy skillet. Fry the fillets for about 5 minutes on each side, until they are golden brown and flake easily when pricked with a fork. Drain on a paper towel and serve immediately. Serves 6.

HARPERS FERRY FILLETS

4 large fish fillets (about
   2 lb.)
salt and pepper
¼ lb. butter

2 lemons, juice only
1 tbsp. dry white wine
¼ cup parmesan cheese
½ tsp. paprika

Salt and pepper the fish fillets. Put the butter in a shallow baking dish in a hot oven (400 to 500 degrees) until it is browned. Place the fillets, flesh side down, in the sizzling hot butter, and bake for 10 or 15 minutes. Turn the fillets with a spatula and baste them with the juice. Sprinkle each piece with lemon juice, dry white wine, parmesan cheese, and paprika. Return them to the oven for about 5 minutes. Place them under the broiler and broil quickly for 1 to 2 minutes. Baste the fish and serve it with the sauce. Serves 4.

SIR ZAYDE'S STEW

1 6-lb. stewing hen, or 2 3-lb. broiler-fryers
2 qt. water
3 large onions, sliced
2 cups cut okra
4 cups fresh diced tomatoes, or 2 16-oz. cans tomatoes
2 cups lima beans
3 medium potatoes, diced
4 cups corn, cut from cob (or 2 16-oz. cans corn)
3 tsp. salt
1 tsp. pepper
1 tbsp. sugar

Cut the chicken in pieces and simmer in the water until the meat can easily be removed from the bones (about 2½ hours). Add the raw vegetables to the broth and simmer, uncovered, until the beans and potatoes are tender. Stir occasionally to prevent scorching. Add the boned and diced chicken and the seasonings. For a thinner stew, increase the water to 3 quarts. If using canned vegetables, include their juices but reduce the amount of water so the total liquid measures 2 quarts for a thick stew, or 3 quarts for a thinner stew. Serves 8 to 10.

LUNTS-MON LAMB CHOPS

2 tbsp. pareve margarine
1 tbsp. minced onion
½ cup sliced mushrooms
3 tbsp. chili sauce
1 tbsp. water
1½ tsp. flour
salt and pepper
8 lamb shoulder steaks

In a skillet, melt the pareve margarine. Add the onion, mushrooms, and chili sauce. Simmer for 5 minutes; then add the flour and water and stir. Salt and pepper the chops and place them in a 12-inch baking dish. Pour the sauce over the chops and bake at 400 degrees for 30 to 35 minutes, or until desired doneness. Serves 4.

BRITISH BRUSSELS SPROUTS
(Microwave)

2 8-oz. pkg. frozen brussels
  sprouts
2 tbsp. water
¼ cup chopped shallots or
  green onions with tops
2 tbsp. butter or margarine

2 tsp. lemon juice
¼ tsp. salt
⅛ tsp. basil
⅛ tsp. oregano
dash pepper

In 1½- to 2-quart casserole, combine the brussels sprouts and water. Cover and microwave on high for 7 to 9 minutes, or until tender, stirring after half the cooking time. Set aside, covered.

Place the shallots (or green onions) and butter (or margarine) in small bowl. Microwave on high for 1½ to 2 minutes, or until the onion is tender. Stir in remaining ingredients.

Drain the brussels sprouts. Pour the onion mixture over the sprouts and stir to coat. Microwave on high for 30 seconds to heat through if needed. Serves 4 to 6.

CALDONIA'S NUTTY CAULIFLOWER

½ cup coarsely chopped
  walnuts
1 tbsp. finely chopped parsley

1 large head cauliflower
¼ cup butter or margarine

Cook cauliflower in boiling water until tender. In a small skillet, melt butter (or margarine). Stir in the walnuts and cook over medium heat until the nuts are slightly browned. Add the chopped parsley, then pour the mixture over the cauliflower. Serve immediately
Serves 6.

MENDEL'S MUSHROOMS

1 lb. mushrooms
3 tbsp. chopped parsley
¼ tsp. chopped garlic
¼ cup bread crumbs
2 tbsp. grated Parmesan
  cheese

salt and pepper
¼ cup olive oil
2 tbsp. Kosher dry white wine

Wash and dry the mushrooms. Place them in a 2-quart baking dish. Sprinkle with parsley, garlic, half of bread crumbs, and grated cheese. Add the salt and pepper to taste. Pour the olive oil and wine over the mixture. Stir once and sprinkle with the rest of the bread crumbs. Bake at 350 degrees for about 20 minutes, or until the mushrooms are tender. Serves 6.

POTOMAC POTATO PUFFS

2 cups mashed potatoes
4 slices crisp fried Beef Frye,
  crumbled
2 eggs, well beaten

1 cup sifted all-purpose flour
2 tsp. baking powder
1 tsp. salt
vegetable oil for deep frying

Combine the potatoes, Beef Frye, and eggs in a bowl. Add the flour, baking powder, and salt. Mix well. Heat the oil in a deep skillet to 375 degrees. Drop by teaspoon into the hot oil. Fry for about 3 minutes or until nicely browned. Drain on absorbent towels. Serves 6.

SQUIRE'S SPINACH SOUFFLE

2 8-oz. pkg. frozen chopped
  spinach
2 eggs, well beaten
¼ tsp. pepper
¼ tsp. garlic powder

1 10½-oz. can condensed
  mushroom soup
¼ cup seasoned bread
  crumbs

Cook the spinach as directed on package. Drain well. Add the beaten eggs, seasoning, and condensed mushroom soup to the spinach. Put the mixture in a greased ring mold or rectangular pyrex dish. Sprinkle with bread crumbs. Bake uncovered, at 350 degrees for 1 hour until browned lightly. Serves 4.

HI! TEA BREAD

½ lb. pitted dates
½ lb. pecans
2 eggs
¾ cup sugar

¾ cup sifted all-purpose flour
pinch salt
½ tsp. baking powder
½ tsp. vanilla extract

Preheat the oven to 300 degrees. Cut the dates in half. Chop pecans coarsely; then set the dates and pecans aside.

Beat the eggs with an electric mixer or food processor. Add the sugar, and beat until the mixture is smooth and thick. Add the flour, salt, and baking powder. Blend, then stir in the dates, chopped pecans, and vanilla with a wooden spoon or rubber spatula. Mix thoroughly. Do not use the processor—the dates and pecans should remain chunky.

Spoon the batter into a greased loaf pan (9½x4½x3 inches) or in a long loaf pan 13x4½x2¼ inches). Cover the pan with foil and bake on the middle shelf of the oven for 1½ hours. Increase the heat to 325 degrees, remove the foil, and continue to bake for another 20 to 30 minutes until a knife inserted into the center of the loaf comes out clean. Cool completely on a rack before slicing. Makes 1 loaf.

JETHRO'S JAM CAKE
(Microwave and Conventional)

1 cup all-purpose flour
1 tsp. cinnamon
¾ tsp. baking soda
¼ tsp. salt
½ cup sugar

⅓ cup vegetable oil
1 egg
¼ cup buttermilk (use ½ cup
   in conventional method)
½ cup red raspberry jam

MICROWAVE: Grease an 8-inch round glass baking dish. In a large bowl, mix the flour, cinnamon, baking soda, and salt together. Combine the sugar, oil, and egg. Add flour mixture and buttermilk to the egg mixture and stir until smooth. Pour the batter into the prepared baking dish. Cover tightly with plastic wrap, turning back one edge to vent. Microwave at 50% power for 5 minutes, rotating the dish twice. Rotate again and microwave at 100% power for 1 to 1½ minutes, or until top of the cake is barely moist when touched. Let stand on a heatproof surface, covered, for 15 minutes. Remove from pan, spread with raspberry jam and serve warm. Serves 6.

CONVENTIONAL: Grease an 8-inch round baking dish. Preheat the oven to 350 degrees. Prepare the cake batter as directed in the microwave method, but increase the buttermilk to ½ cup. Bake for 20 to 25 minutes at 350 degrees, or until a knife inserted in center comes out clean. Cool in the pan on a wire rack for 15 minutes. Remove from pan, spread with raspberry jam and serve warm. Serves 6.

LADY ANNE'S APPLE PUDDING

2 qt. peeled apple slices
1½ cups all-purpose flour
1 tbsp. baking powder
½ tsp. salt
½ cup butter or margarine

1 cup sugar, divided
1 egg
¾ cup water
½ tsp. cinnamon

Arrange the apples in a 2-quart glass baking dish. Sift the flour, baking powder, and salt together. Cream the butter or margarine; then add ¾ cup of the sugar gradually, beating well. Beat in the egg. Add the flour mixture alternately with the water and beat until smooth. Pour the batter over the apples. Blend the remaining sugar with the cinnamon and sprinkle it over the batter. Bake at 375 degrees for 45 minutes, or until the pudding tests done. Serve warm. Serves 8.

MAYS CORN MUFFINS

1 cup white cornmeal
1 cup all-purpose flour
1 tsp. salt
3 tsp. baking powder

2 tbsp. sugar
2 eggs, lightly beaten
1 cup milk
3 tbsp. butter, melted

Preheat the oven to 400°. Grease muffin tins that are 1½ inches in diameter.

Sift the dry ingredients into a mixing bowl. Combine the eggs, milk, and melted butter; then add them to the dry ingredients, mixing just until blended. Do not overmix. Spoon the batter into the greased muffin tins, filling each tin completely full. Bake at 400° for 20 minutes, or until done. Yields 1½ dozen muffins.

Arkansas is well and alive with a secure future. Just look into its past to see where it came from, and you will view a land of opportunity with a prosperous present and a promising future. Also alive and well in Arkansas is the Old South. The landscapes, the antebellum homes, the accents, and the hospitality are enchanting.

Overall, Arkansas can best be described as Mother Nature at her best: mountain beauty, pastoral scenes, and historic sites. People, still clinging to their small town simplicity, live side-by-side with big city sophisticates. Two-thirds of its people are rural, and farming is still the chief occupation.

Underground, Arkansas has remained a source of great mineral wealth, producing bauxite, stone, gravel, sand, diamonds, and natural gases. Miles of fishing lakes and streams and forests that cover almost two-thirds of the area have made their contributions to the state's economy. These diverse physical features exist nowhere else; and the state deservedly has been named the Natural State.

Hernando De Soto, in the mid-1500s, still seeking his fountain of youth, journeyed far into the Ozarks to the present site of Hot Springs, Arkansas. The hot springs probably were the origin of the legend of the fountain of youth. More than a century later, two Frenchmen, Father Jacques Marquette and Louis Joliet, while exploring the Mississippi River, landed at the mouth of the Arkansas River. However, it was not until Spain ceded the territory to France that settlement began. The first permanent settlement, the Arkansas Post, was built by Henri de Tonti in 1686. It was actually the first white settlement in the lower Mississippi Valley.

During the growing period, Arkansas was included in the area that France ceded to Spain. When Spain took possession of the region in 1769, it renamed Arkansas Post as Fort Charles III.

In the early 1800s, cotton was grown commercially and several fur trading posts were established along the waterways. Nevertheless, much of the land still remained unsettled. By the time the homesteaders flocked into Arkansas, the state had been through several transitions. It had been a part of the Louisiana Purchase, became the Arkansas Territory, and finally entered the Union as the 25th state. It was admitted as a slave state because the slave system was well established in the cotton-growing region.

The California Gold Rush in 1849 brought thousands of prospectors through the territory, buying supplies and taking overland stages to the West. Situated midway on the route to California, the state became a center of bustling towns. Arkansas was on its way to a population explosion and prosperity.

When the Civil War began, Arkansas was undecided as to which side it would join. Although slavery existed in the state, the sympathies of the people were evenly divided between the Union and Confederacy. In May of 1861, the Arkansas convention voted to remain in the Union. However, when President Lincoln called for volunteers, the convention met again. This time it adopted the Secession Act, making Arkansas the ninth state to join the Confederacy.

At the end of the Civil War, Confederate men cooperated to establish a Union government, and Arkansas was readmitted to the Union in 1868. Reconstruction was slow and difficult; but as the building of the railroads became a viable industry, economic expansion began anew in Arkansas. The state progressed steadily, leaving behind the poverty and destruction caused by the war.

As Arkansas entered the twentieth century, the future looked bright. Much of Arkansas' natural resources were developed. Little Rock remained the state capital. Leaders surveyed all of the state's resources with foresight and embarked on an industrial expansion program that would secure the economic future of Arkansas.

From the indescribable beauty of the River Valley to the majestic panorama of the Ozarks; from the Timberlands to the Delta; from the Ouachita Mountains ablaze with wild flowers to the famous hot springs; Arkansas is a kaleidoscope of scenic wonders, old folkways, outdoor adventures and festive events.

Indeed, Arkansas has lived up to its other nicknames—the Wonder State and the Land of Opportunity. Explore its natural wonders, enjoy its historic past, relax in the serenity of the landscape, and feast on farm-grown vegetables and freshly baked breads, pies, and cakes. There is no end to the pleasure you'll derive from being an "Arkansas Traveler."

WAFLERS

Mix a cup and a half of thick yeast with a little warm milk, and set it with two pounds of flour before the fire to rise, then mix with them one pound of fresh butter, ten eggs, a grated nutmeg, a quarter of a pint of orange flowerwater, a little powdered cinnamon, and three pints of warm milk; when the batter is perfectly smooth, butter the irons, fill them with it, close them down tightly, and put them between the bars of a bright clear fire; when sufficiently done, they will slip easily out of the irons.

Wafler irons are required and can be obtained at any good ironmongers of the Hebrew persuasion.

FAMILY FRUIT PUNCH

1 cup water
1½ cups sugar
½ cup lemon juice
1 cup orange juice

½ cup grated pineapple
½ cup pineapple syrup
½ cup apricot syrup

Heat sugar and water, stirring until dissolved. Allow to cool then add the other ingredients. Serve over crushed ice. Serves 4.

CULPEPPER'S PICKLED PEACHES

2 lb. sugar
2 cups vinegar
2 sticks cinnamon

2 tbsp. whole cloves
4 qt. peaches, peeled

Boil the sugar, vinegar, and spices for 20 minutes. Drop the peeled fruit in, a few at a time, and cook until tender. Pack in hot, sterilized jars, adding syrup to within ½ inch of the top; seal. Makes 4 quarts.

METSIEH MUSHROOMS
(Microwave and Conventional)

12 medium-sized mushrooms
(about 1½ inches in
diameter)
salt
½ cup minced corned beef
2 tbsp. finely chopped
shallots

1 tbsp. prepared mustard
2 tsp. mayonnaise
dash pepper
3 or 4 pimiento-stuffed green
olives, sliced

MICROWAVE: Wipe the mushrooms gently with damp cloth. Remove the stems carefully and reserve for another purpose. Place the mushroom caps, rounded side down, around the edge of large microwave-safe dinner plate. Sprinkle very lightly with salt. Combine the corned beef, shallots, mustard, mayonnaise, and pepper. Spoon the mixture into the mushroom caps. Microwave at 100% power for 3 minutes, rotating the plate once. Let stand for 2 minutes. Top with olive slices. Arrange on a platter and serve immediately. Makes 12 appetizers.

CONVENTIONAL: Preheat the oven to 375°. Prepare mushrooms and corned beef mixture as directed in the microwave method. Spoon the corned beef mixture into the mushrooms and place in an 8-inch baking dish. Bake 12 minutes. Top with olive slices, arrange on platter and serve immediately. Makes 12 appetizers.

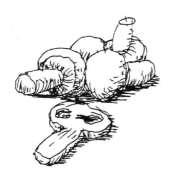

A RELISH TO RELISH

8 large onions, chopped
10 sweet red peppers,
  chopped

1 cup sugar
1 qt. white vinegar
4 tsp. salt

Combine all ingredients in a kettle and bring the mixture to a full boil. Turn heat down to medium and cook until the mixture is somewhat thickened (about 45 minutes to 1 hour). Stir occasionally to prevent the relish from sticking to the kettle. Ladle the hot relish into hot, sterilized half-pint jars. Adjust the jar lids and process in a water-bath canner for 5 minutes. Complete seals, if necessary, after removing jars from canner. Makes 2½ pints.

MASSA'S MOLASSES BREAD

1 cup plus 2 tbsp. flour
1 cup cornmeal
½ tsp. salt
2½ tsp. baking powder
1 level tsp. baking soda

2 eggs, beaten
1½ cups buttermilk
3 tbsp. melted butter
4 tbsp. dark unsulfured
  molasses

Combine the flour, cornmeal, salt, baking powder, and baking soda. Add the beaten eggs to the buttermilk, butter, and molasses. Blend. Add the egg mixture gradually to the dry ingredients, beating well after each addition. Pour into a shallow, buttered baking dish. Bake in a 400° oven for 35 minutes, or until firm and golden brown. Cool. Cut into squares; serve topped with molasses butter.

Molasses Butter

¼ lb. sweet butter
3 tbsp. molasses

Soften the sweet butter; then whip it with a rotary beater until light and fluffy. Gradually add the molasses. Blend well.

MOUNTAIN VALLEY BREAD

3 ripe bananas
1 egg
⅓ cup sugar
2 tbsp. light molasses
2 tbsp. melted shortening

2 cups sifted flour
1 tsp. baking powder
1 tsp. baking soda
½ tsp. salt
1 cup chopped pecans

Mash the bananas until no lumps remain. Add the unbeaten egg. Mix well. Beat in the sugar, molasses, and shortening. Sift together the flour, baking powder, baking soda, and salt. Add the flour mixture to banana-egg mixture. Stir in the pecans. Bake in a greased 9x5x3-inch loaf pan at 325 degrees for about 1 hour, or until a cake tester comes out clean. Makes 1 loaf.

ERLEE'S ENGLISH PEA SALAD

1 16-oz. can English peas, drained
1 cup diced cheddar cheese
½ cup chopped sweet pickle

½ cup mayonnaise
3 hard-cooked eggs, diced
½ cup chopped bell pepper
2 tbsp. chopped pimiento

Mix together all ingredients thoroughly. Chill and serve. Serves 8.

ARKANSAS KRACKER BALLS

2 tbsp. pareve margarine
1 egg
2 tbsp. chopped parsley
8 tbsp. cracker meal or
  cracker crumbs

salt and pepper to taste
2 tbsp. beef or chicken soup
  stock

Cream the pareve margarine. Add the egg, parsley, cracker meal, seasonings, and soup stock. Mix well. Place the mixture in the refrigerator until chilled. When chilled, form into balls the size of small marbles. Drop the balls into boiling salted water and cook for about 10 minutes. Serve in any kind of soup. Yields about 12 to 16 balls.

OZARK BROWN CABBAGE SOUP

3- to 4-pound soup bone
2 qt. cold water
2 tsp. salt
¼ tsp. pepper
1 bay leaf

½ medium head cabbage
2 medium onions, sliced
1 cup chopped celery
1 cup chopped beet tops
1 tbsp. vegetable oil

Cover the bone with water and add the salt, pepper, and bay leaf. Heat to boiling; then cook for 1½ hours. Cut the cabbage into eighths and sauté with remaining vegetables in the vegetable oil. Brown well. Add the vegetables to the stock and bone and continue cooking for 45 minutes. Remove meat from the soup bone and add it to the soup. Serves 8.

BEEFIN' BEAN BOWL

1½ lb. ground beef
½ cup ketchup
½ tsp. dry mustard
2 tbsp. vinegar
3 tbsp. dark brown sugar
1 small onion, minced

1 16-oz can green lima beans
1 16-oz. can red kidney beans
1 16-oz. can vegetarian baked
  beans
½ tsp. salt

Brown the meat in a large skillet. Add the remaining ingredients and mix well. Pour the mixture into a large 2½- to 3-quart casserole dish. Bake at 350 degrees for 30 minutes. Serves 8.

CHICKEN CRITTER 'N RICE
(Microwave)

1 medium onion, chopped
1 cup chopped green pepper
1 tbsp. olive oil
2 cups quick-cooking rice
1¾ cups tomato juice
1 cup frozen peas
⅓ cup chopped stuffed olives

1 tsp. sugar
½ tsp. salt
⅛ tsp. pepper
5 to 6 drops Tabasco sauce
2- to 2½-pound broiler-fryer
  chicken pieces
¼ tsp. paprika

In a 12x8-inch dish, combine the onion, green pepper, and olive oil. Microwave on high for 3½ minutes, or until tender. Stir in all ingredients, except for the chicken and paprika. Arrange the chicken on top, bony side up and the meatiest portions toward the outer edges of the dish. Cover with plastic wrap.

Microwave on high for 10 minutes; then turn over, rearrange the chicken and rotate the dish. Sprinkle with paprika. Cover and microwave on high for 7 to 10 minutes, or until the meat is no longer pink and the rice is tender. Serves 4.

SHAH! SHAH! SALMON CROQUETTES

1 7¾-oz. can salmon, drained and flaked
½ cup soft bread crumbs
¼ cup chopped onion
¼ cup chopped green pepper
1 tbsp. diced pimiento
1 egg, slightly beaten
¼ tsp. salt
¼ tsp. black pepper
1 tbsp. vegetable oil

In a large mixing bowl, combine the salmon, bread crumbs, onion, green pepper, pimiento, egg, salt, and pepper. Mix well; then form into 4 patties.

In a 10-inch skillet, heat the oil. Add the patties and brown them for 4 to 5 minutes on each side. Serves 4.

DILLY OF A CARROT
(Microwave and Conventional)

1 lb. carrots, sliced or cut into julienne strips
2 tbsp. butter or margarine
1 tsp. dill
½ tsp. salt
dash freshly ground pepper
1 tbsp. water (for microwave method) or ¼ cup water (for conventional method)

MICROWAVE: Combine the carrots, butter or margarine, dill, salt, pepper, and 1 tablespoon of water in a 1½-quart glass bowl. Cover it tightly with plastic wrap, turning back one edge to vent. Microwave at 100% power for 6 minutes, stirring once. Let stand, covered, for 2 minutes. Stir and spoon into a serving dish. Serves 4 to 6.

CONVENTIONAL: Place the carrots and ¼ cup of water in a 2-quart saucepan. Heat to boiling. Reduce heat, cover, and simmer for 8 minutes or until tender. Drain. Add butter or margarine, dill, salt, and pepper. Let stand until the butter melts. Stir lightly and spoon into a serving dish. Serves 4 to 6.

EUREKA! ENGLISH PEAS

3 tbsp. butter,
1 tbsp. flour
1 cup milk
2 egg yolks
1 16-oz. can English peas
1 tbsp. grated onion

1 tbsp. sugar
salt and pepper to taste
½ bell pepper
1 tbsp. chopped pimiento
1 tbsp. chopped celery

Make a sauce by melting 1 tablespoon of the butter then combining it with the flour, milk, and egg yolks. Set aside.

Drain and mash the peas. Add 1 tablespoon of the butter, grated onion, sugar, salt and pepper. Brown the bell pepper in the remaining tablespoon of butter. Add the browned pepper, chopped pimiento, and chopped celery to the mashed pea mixture. Combine the pea mixture and the milk sauce, then bake in a 300-degree oven for 45 minutes. Serves 4.

GREEN BEANS GENUG

1 medium onion, minced
3 tbsp. vegetable shortening
3½ cups cooked green beans
1 16-oz. can stewed tomatoes

½ tbsp. sugar
1 tsp. salt
2 tsp. lemon juice
⅛ tsp. pepper

Sauté the onion in vegetable shortening until tender, about 3 to 4 minutes. Add the beans, stewed tomatoes with liquid, sugar, salt, lemon juice, and pepper. Heat thoroughly, stirring occasionally. Serves 8.

PRAIRIE PECAN POTATOES

1 tbsp. margarine
1 tbsp. minced onion
1 tbsp. chopped green pepper
2 eggs, beaten
1½ cup unseasoned mashed
  potatoes
1 cup pecans, chopped

1 tbsp. chopped parsley
½ tsp. salt
dash pepper
¼ tsp. Worcestershire sauce
fine dry bread crumbs
1 tbsp. water

Heat the margarine in a skillet, then sauté the onion and green pepper until lightly browned. Combine 1 egg, mashed potatoes, pecans, salt, pepper, and Worcestershire sauce. Shape into croquettes. Roll the croquettes in the bread crumbs. Beat the remaining egg with the tablespoon of water, dip the croquettes in the mixture, then roll them in bread crumbs again. Let stand 10 minutes to dry. Fry until golden brown in oil heated to 375 degrees. Serves 8.

A CRUMMY CRACKER PUDDING

⅔ cup cracker crumbs
¾ cup sugar
½ tsp. salt
4 cups milk, scalded
¼ cup melted shortening

2 eggs, separated
1 tsp. vanilla extract
¼ cup confectioners' sugar
1 tbsp. lemon juice

Combine the cracker crumbs, sugar, salt, and milk. Stir in the melted shortening and beaten egg yolks. Add the vanilla. Pour the mixture into a greased baking dish, then bake in moderate oven (325 degrees) for 1 hour.

Beat the whites of the eggs until stiff, adding confectioners' sugar gradually, then add the lemon juice. Remove the dish from the oven and cover with meringue. Bake in slow oven (300 degrees) until meringue is brown, about 20 to 30 minutes. Serves 6.

MOCK MINTZ PIE

2 cups chopped tart apples
1 cup raisins
1 cup brown sugar
⅛ tsp. cinnamon
⅛ tsp. nutmeg

⅛ tsp. salt
1 cup thick sour cream
1 double unbaked 9-inch pie
  pastry
1 tsp. flour

Preheat oven to 450 degrees. Mix apples, raisins, sugar, spices, salt, and sour cream together. Line a 9-inch pie pan with the pastry and dust it with flour. Pour in the filling and cover with the top crust. Bake at 450 degrees for 10 minutes. Reduce the temperature to 350 degrees; bake for 45 minutes, or until apples are tender. Serve hot. Yields one 9-inch pie.

RIVKE'S RICE TARTS

¾ cup uncooked rice
1½ pints milk
½ tsp. salt
4 egg yolks
1 cup sugar
3 tbsp. orange juice

1 tbsp. lemon juice
1 cup heavy cream, whipped
8 individual baked pastry
  shells
cinnamon

Wash the rice in cold water. In a saucepan, heat the milk; then add the salt and rice. Cook slowly until the rice is tender, stirring occasionally. Beat the egg yolks, add the sugar, and combine with the cooked rice. Cook 1 more minute. Cool.

Fold the orange juice, lemon juice, and whipped cream into the cooled rice mixture. Fill baked pastry shells with the mixture, sprinkle with cinnamon, then brown under the broiler. Top with additional whipped cream, if desired. Serves 8.

UNDERGROUND CHOCOLATE PIE

2 squares baking chocolate
2½ cups milk, divided
¾ cup sugar
3 tbsp. cornstarch
3 tbsp. flour
½ tsp. salt

2 egg yolks, well beaten
1 tsp. vanilla
1 9-inch baked pie shell
3 egg whites
6 tbsp. sugar

Grate or cut the chocolate into 2 cups of the milk. Place in a double broiler over hot water to melt. Combine the sugar, cornstarch, flour, and salt; then blend with remaining ½ cup of milk.

When the chocolate is melted and the milk is scalded, add the beaten egg yolks. Stir constantly. Add the flour and sugar mixture. Continue to cook over boiling water, stirring constantly, until thick. Add the vanilla and allow to cool. Place in pastry shell. Beat the egg whites until foamy; then add the sugar gradually while beating until stiff peaks form. Spread over pie. Bake in a 300° oven for about 7 minutes, or until meringue is lightly brown. Yields: 1 9-inch pie.

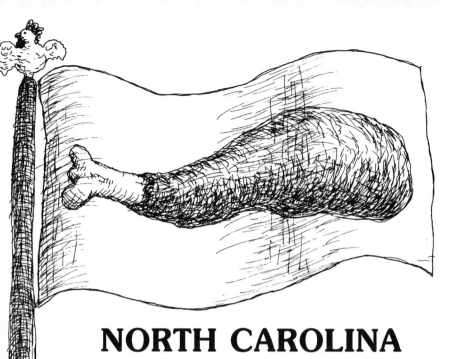

NORTH CAROLINA
The Tar Heel State

Just south of what is now Virginia was a prolific wilderness waiting to be discovered—North Carolina. The dawning came in 1584 when Queen Elizabeth I granted Sir Walter Raleigh the right to colonize America. On his first expedition, he explored Roanoke Island and returned to England with encouraging reports of a fertile land worth settling. Raleigh made another expedition in 1585, bringing with him a group of eager settlers, and Roanoke Island became the first English colony in America. However, it was abandoned in 1586.

Sir Walter Raleigh established a second colony in 1587. That was the same year that Virginia Dare was born at Roanoke Island—the first child born to English parents in America. After helping the more than one hundred settlers build a fort and plow the fields, Raleigh returned to England, promising to send back much-needed supplies and more colonists. However, England's concerns turned toward the threats of the Spanish Armada, so it was three years before a ship returned to Roanoke Island. The crew found an abandoned colony— settlers gone, tools and weapons rusting on the ground, and the fort surrounded by high grass. The word "CROATOAN" carved on a tree was the only clue as to what may have happened. To this day, although legends abound, the fate of the "Lost Colony" has never been learned. It remains a romantic mystery of early America.

By the mid-1600s, the first permanent settlement had been established and the territory that is now North Carolina and South Carolina was granted by Charles I. It was called *Carolana* which means "the land of Charles." Charles II extended the Carolina territory and, in 1663, granted the Carolina region to eight lord proprietors. The colony prospered, but the settlers soon became discontent and continually quarreled with the proprietors over feudal laws.

Unable to cope with the constant unrest and angry colonists, seven proprietors sold their shares of Carolina territory back to the king in 1729. North Carolina and South Carolina were divided into separate provinces. North Carolina was one of the first regions of the New World to be settled by the English, and it was the first colony to vote for independence from England in 1776.

During the Revolutionary War, the British had their biggest victory in North Carolina at the Guilford Courthouse. However, heavy

English losses helped force Lord Cornwallis to surrender at Yorktown. Cornwallis is often credited with the nicknaming of North Carolina. The sobriquet, the Tar Heel State, supposedly dates back to the time when Cornwallis' troops, upon crossing a river in which tar had been spilled, left their heel marks on the banks.

Immediately following the war, North Carolina refused to ratify the new Constitution. When the Bill of Rights was introduced in Congress and accepted by North Carolina, they entered the Union as the twelfth state in 1789. That same year, the University of North Carolina was granted a charter, becoming the first state university in the country. It opened its doors in January 1795.

The 1800s saw rapid development in the Carolina region. Canals, roads, and railroads solved the problems of carrying goods from the seacoast to the interior. These developments would play an important role in the Civil War. Dependent upon slave labor for their lucrative tobacco industry, North Carolina sided with the Confederacy and became one of the last states to secede from the Union on May 20, 1861.

The Civil War drained North Carolina, economically and physically. The state supplied over 125,000 troops to the Confederate army—more than any other state. North Carolina's ports and railroads played an important role in getting supplies to the Confederate forces and, as such, were under constant siege. General Sherman and his army invaded North Carolina in March of 1865, and a month later, General Johnston was forced to surrender at a farmstead called Bennett Place, just seven miles from Durham. It was one of the most significant events in the history of our nation: the final surrender of the armies of the Carolinas, Georgia, and Florida. The war was concluded.

North Carolina survived the bitter and violent struggle for survival during the Reconstruction period. Through perseverance and determination, the wealth of the state steadily increased. Manufacturing of tobacco, textiles, and furniture paired with improvement in education, industry, roads, and farming to aid in the state's progression.

The capital city of Raleigh is an example of North Carolina's rich and diverse history. Selected as the state capital in 1788, laid out in

1792, incorporated in 1795, occupied by General Sherman in 1865—it surmounted all adversities and remains the capital today.

The people of North Carolina are as diverse as the state's many regions. Yet the farmers of the Low Country, the laborers and townspeople of the Piedmont, and the mountain folk and the miners in the Valley are all held together by the bond of state pride. North Carolina has kept its scenic charm and the people still cling to the tradition of life in a bygone era. With all the fast changes and modern growth, one very old tradition remains in practice—genuine hospitality. North Carolinians extend invitations to share and enjoy the simple pleasure of their company, their hearty family meals, and an added wish to just let that old "Carolina moon keep shining."

A SAVOURY PIE FOR PERSONS OF DELICATE DIGESTION.

Cut up fowl and sweetbread, lay in the dish in alternate layers with meat, jelly, and the yolks of hard-boiled eggs without the whites, and flavor with lemon-juice, white pepper, and salt; cover with rice prepared as follows: boil half a pound of rice in sufficient water to permit it to swell; when tender beat it up to a thick paste with the yolk of one or two eggs, season with a little salt, and spread it over the dish thickly. The fowl and sweetbread should have been previously simmered till half done in a little weak broth; the pie must be baked in a gentle oven, and if the rice will not brown sufficiently, finish with a salamander.

BEAUFORT BROCCOLI DIP

1 10-oz. pkg. frozen chopped broccoli
2 ribs celery, chopped
1 large onion, chopped
¾ stick margarine
1 4-oz. can mushroom stems and pieces, drained
1 10¾-ounce can condensed mushroom soup
6 oz. shredded mozzarella cheese
1 tsp. garlic powder
2 tbsp. Worcestershire sauce

Cook broccoli according to package directions. Drain. Sauté the celery and onions in the margarine. Add the mushrooms and cook until tender. Over low to medium heat, warm the soup and shredded cheese until the cheese is melted. Add the garlic powder and stir frequently. Add the broccoli, the sautéed mixture, and Worcestershire sauce. Stir gently to blend. Serve warm with crackers or chips. Makes about 6 cups.

APPALACHIAN APPLE BUTTER

24 medium apples, quartered
and peeled (about 6 lb.)
2 qt. sweet cider

3 cups sugar
1½ tsp. cinnamon
½ tsp. cloves

Cook the apples in the cider until tender. Press through a sieve or food mill. Measure 3 quarts of apple pulp. Cook the pulp until it is thick enough to round up in a spoon. As the pulp thickens, stir it to prevent sticking.

Add the sugar and spices. Cook slowly for about 1 hour, stirring frequently until thick. Pour the hot mixture into hot pint jars, leaving ¼ inch of head space. Adjust the caps. Process pints for 10 minutes in boiling water bath. Makes about 5 pints.

YESHIVA YAM BISCUITS

2 cups flour
⅔ cup sugar
2 tbsp. baking powder
1½ tsp. salt

½ cup vegetable shortening
2 cups mashed cooked sweet
potatoes
¼ cup milk

Sift the flour, sugar, baking powder, and salt together into a bowl. Cut in the shortening until mixture is the consistency of cornmeal. Stir in the sweet potatoes and milk. Turn the dough out on a floured board and knead lightly. Roll out to ½-inch thickness and cut with biscuit cutter. Place on a greased cookie sheet. Bake at 425° for 12 to 15 minutes. Makes 2 dozen biscuits.

IT'S HOT! POTATO SALAD

**6 medium-size potatoes
(about 2 lb.)
1 cup finely chopped onion**

**3 tbsp. finely chopped parsley
salt and pepper to taste**

Wash the potatoes; then cook covered in boiling salted water for 20 to 30 minutes, or until the potatoes are tender when pierced with a fork. Drain. Dry the potatoes by shaking pan over low heat. Peel, cut into ¼-inch slices, and put into a bowl. Add the onion, parsley, salt, and pepper. Toss together lightly. Pour the dressing over the potato mixture and toss lightly to coat evenly. Warm the salad in a large skillet over low heat for 10 to 15 minutes, until potatoes are heated. Serve immediately. Serves 6.

Dressing

**⅔ cup cider vinegar
⅓ cup water
1½ tsp. sugar**

**1 egg
⅓ cup salad oil**

In a small saucepan, mix together the vinegar, water, and sugar. Heat to boiling. Beat the egg slightly. Continue beating while gradually adding the vinegar mixture. Add the salad oil gradually while beating constantly until mixture is well blended. Makes about 1½ cups of dressing.

LIZA'S LIMA BEAN SALAD

2 cups cooked lima beans   **1 tbsp. chopped chives**
1 tbsp. chopped pimiento

Lightly toss together the beans, pimiento, and chives. Add the dressing and toss lightly together until all beans are coated with dressing. Set in refrigerator to chill for at least 1 hour. Serves 4.

Dressing

⅔ cup thick sour cream   **1 tsp. sugar**
1 tbsp. wine vinegar   **¾ tsp. salt**
2 tsp. lemon juice   **⅛ tsp. white pepper**

Mix together the sour cream, vinegar, and lemon juice. Add the sugar, salt, and white pepper and mix well. Makes about 1 cup of dressing.

QUE-CUMBER SOUP

2 lb. cucumbers   **1 green pepper, chopped**
salt and pepper   **1 tbsp. melted butter**
½ cup hot water   **2 cups light cream**
1 medium onion, chopped   **2 tbsp. chopped parsley**
1 clove garlic, minced

Peel and chop the cucumbers; then place them in a large saucepan. Add the salt, pepper, water, onion, garlic, and green pepper and cook until cucumbers are tender. Remove from heat and cool. Place in a blender or food processor and blend until pureed. Stir in the butter and light cream. Serve hot or cold garnished with parsley. Serves 6.

TUNOODLES
(Microwave and Conventional)

1 10½-oz. can condensed mushroom soup
½ cup milk
2 cups cooked egg noodles
1 cup cooked peas
2 tbsp. chopped pimiento
2 6½-oz cans tuna, drained and flaked
1 tbsp. butter
2 tbsp. bread crumbs

MICROWAVE: In a 2-quart microwave-safe casserole, combine the soup and milk; then stir in the noodles, peas, pimiento, and tuna. Cover and microwave on high for 9 minutes, or until hot, stirring at 3-minute intervals.

In a small saucepan, heat the butter. Stir the bread crumbs into the hot butter until lightly browned. Sprinkle over noodle mixture. Serves 4.

CONVENTIONAL: In 1½-quart casserole, combine the soup and milk; then stir in noodles, peas, pimiento, and tuna. Bake in a 400° oven for 25 minutes. Meanwhile, in small saucepan, heat the butter. Stir the bread crumbs into the hot butter until lightly browned. Top the casserole with buttered bread crumbs and bake for an additional 5 minutes. Serves 4.

CHAPEL HILL CHICKEN PIE

2 chicken breasts, bones and skin removed
3 slices Beef Frye, cut into small strips
12 thin slices Kosher smoked sausage
¼ cup minced onion
¼ cup minced green onion
1 tbsp. minced garlic
2 tbsp. minced green bell pepper

3 tbsp. flour
1 tsp. basil
¼ cup Kosher condensed chicken soup
¼ cup Kosher white wine
salt and pepper
1 9-inch pie crust
1 egg, beaten with 1 tbsp. water

Heat the oven to 350°. Cut the chicken into small pieces. Cook the Beef Frye slowly in a pan until crisp; then remove to paper towels. Add onions, green onions, garlic, and bell pepper to the Beef Frye drippings (add a bit of oil if there is not enough). Cook for 2 minutes; then add the chicken and sausage. Cook for 5 minutes, or until the chicken is cooked.

Add the flour and cook, stirring, for 3 minutes. Add the basil, chicken soup, and wine. Bring to a boil, then reduce the heat. Pour into a baking dish and cover with the pie pastry. Brush with the beaten egg mixture, and bake until brown (about 15 to 20 minutes). Serves 4.

OUR OVEN BBQ CHICKEN

1 fryer chicken (2½ to 3 pounds), cut in serving pieces

3 cups Our Oven BBQ Sauce (see recipe)

Heat the oven to 400°. Place the chicken, skin side up, in a well-oiled pan. Do not overlap the pieces. Brush with Our Oven BBQ Sauce; then bake uncovered for 40 to 50 minutes. Baste with sauce at 10-minute intervals. Place on a hot platter; then pour the sauce from the pan over the chicken. Serves 4.

OUR OVEN BBQ SAUCE

¾ cup chopped onion　　　　3 tbsp. sugar
½ cup vegetable oil　　　　 3 tbsp. Worcestershire sauce
¾ cup ketchup　　　　　　 2 tbsp. prepared mustard
¾ cup water　　　　　　　 2 tsp. salt
⅓ cup lemon juice　　　　　½ tsp. pepper

Cook onion in the hot vegetable oil until soft. Add the remaining ingredients. Simmer 15 minutes. Makes about 3½ cups of sauce (enough to baste 2 small broiler chickens or 1 fryer).

CALABASH CHOPS
(Microwave)

½ cup chopped onion　　　　　　1 tbsp. lemon juice
4 veal rib chops, 1½ inches　　　 ¼ tsp. dry mustard
　thick　　　　　　　　　　　⅛ tsp allspice
⅔ cup ketchup　　　　　　　　 ⅛ tsp. pepper
½ cup brown sugar

Place the chopped onion in a 12x8-inch glass baking dish. Microwave on high for 1½ to 2½ minutes, or until tender. Arrange the chops over the onion with the meatiest portions to the outside of the dish.

Combine the remaining ingredients in a small bowl. Spoon half of the mixture over the chops. Microwave on high for 3 minutes. Reduce power to 50% (medium) for 7 to 12 minutes, or until the meat is done to degree desired. Serves 4.

STONE MOUNTAIN STEAK

½ cup flour
2 tsp. salt
⅛ tsp. pepper
2 lb. shoulder steak, 1 inch
thick

2 tbsp. vegetable oil
2 medium onions, chopped
¼ cup water
1 16-oz. can tomatoes or 2
cups fresh tomatoes

Combine the flour, salt, and pepper; then pound it into both sides of the meat with a sharp-edged meat pounder. Heat the vegetable oil in a large, heavy fry pan. Brown the meat for about 10 minutes on each side. Remove meat from pan.

Cook the onions in the oil until golden. Stir in the remaining flour mixture from dredging meat. Add the water and tomatoes and cook, stirring, until boiling. Return meat to fry pan. Reduce heat, cover, and simmer for 1½ to 2 hours until very tender. Serve on a hot platter, pouring the gravy over the meat. Serves 4 to 5.

CRABBY WILD RICE

½ lb. wild rice
1 can condensed mushroom
soup
½ cup light cream

1½ lb. flaked smoked trout
2 4-oz. cans mushrooms,
drained
1 cup grated colby cheese

Cook the rice according to the package directions. Dilute the soup with the cream. Layer the rice, smoked trout, soup mixture, mushrooms, and cheese in a greased casserole. Cover and bake at 350° for 30 minutes. Uncover and bake until the cheese is melted. Serves 8.

SUPPER FROM THE STREAM
(Microwave)

2 medium potatoes, scrubbed
and diced
1 large carrot, halved lengthwise and cut crosswise in
thin slices
1 small onion, chopped fine
1 medium rib celery, diced
1½ tbsp. butter or margarine
1 tbsp. lemon-pepper
seasonings
4 4-oz. flounder fillets
1 tbsp. lemon juice
½ medium green bell
pepper, diced
1 medium ripe tomato, diced

Place the potatoes in a 9-inch-square, microwave-safe baking dish. Scatter the carrot, onion, and celery on top. Melt the butter or margarine in a 1-cup glass measure. Stir in the lemon-pepper. Pour half of the butter mixture over the vegetables in the baking dish. Cover with vented plastic wrap. Microwave on high for 10 to 12 minutes, stirring once, until the potatoes are almost tender. Let stand covered for 2 minutes.

Arrange the fish on top of the vegetables, with the thickest parts toward outside edge of the dish. Sprinkle the lemon juice over the fish; then drizzle the remaining butter mixture and scatter the bell pepper on top. Cover with vented plastic wrap. Microwave on high for 4 to 5 minutes, rotating the dish ½ turn once. When the fish is almost opaque in thickest part when tested with the top of small knife, scatter the tomato over top. Cover and microwave for 1 minute. Let stand 2 to 3 minutes. Serves 4.

ODESSEE'S OKRA

1 lb. young okra
boiling salted water
½ cup cornmeal
dash cayenne pepper

½ tsp. salt
⅛ tsp. black pepper
oil for frying

Cut off the stem end and tip of the okra pods. Wash thoroughly. Cook in boiling salted water for 8 minutes. Drain and dry completely. Combine the cornmeal with the cayenne pepper, salt, and black pepper. Roll the okra in seasoned cornmeal. Fry in deep hot oil (350 degrees) until brown. Drain on paper towels. Serve immediately. Serves 6.

PINEAPPLED CARROTS

1 8-oz. can pineapple chunks
  and juice
¼ cup packed brown sugar
1 tbsp. butter or pareve
  margarine

2 tsp. cornstarch
½ tsp. ground cinnamon
1 16-oz. can whole carrots,
  drained

In a saucepan, combine the pineapple juice, sugar, butter (or pareve margarine), cornstarch, and cinnamon. Cook over medium heat and stir until clear and thickened. Add the pineapple chunks and carrots. Heat and serve immediately. Serves 4 to 6.

RALEIGH'S ROASTED POTATOES

12 tiny new potatoes, halved
  (or 4 medium potatoes,
  cut into eighths)
2 large shallots (or 4 green
  onions), finely chopped

2 tbsp. vegetable oil
dash salt

In a 13x9x2-inch baking dish, combine the cut potatoes and shallots. Pour the vegetable oil over the potatoes; toss gently to coat. Sprinkle lightly with salt. Bake, uncovered, in a 450° oven for about 25 minutes or until the potatoes are tender and light brown. Serves 4.

TAR HEEL TOMATOES WITH ZUCCHINI

¼ cup vegetable oil
1 clove garlic, minced
4 to 5 medium zucchini
¼ tsp. oregano
¼ tsp. basil
4 to 5 medium ripe tomatoes

½ cup Kosher bread crumbs
2 tbsp. melted butter or
  pareve margarine
¾ cup shredded cheddar
  cheese (optional)

Heat the oil in a large skillet. Cut the zucchini into ¼-inch slices. Add the garlic and zucchini slices to the hot oil and sauté for a few minutes. Remove from the heat and set aside.

Combine the oregano and basil. Peel the tomatoes and cut them into slices. In a greased, 1½-quart casserole dish, alternate layers of sautéed zucchini, seasonings, cheese (if desired), and tomato slices. Repeat layers. Add the bread crumbs to the melted butter (or pareve margarine) and sprinkle over the casserole. Bake, uncovered, in a 350° oven for 30 minutes, or until top is nicely browned. Serves 6.

BLUE RIDGE BERRY PIE

4 cups fresh blueberries
1¼ cups water, divided
1 cup sugar
3 tbsp. cornstarch
juice of ½ lemon

1 cup heavy cream
additional sugar to taste
1 baked 9-inch pie shell,
cooled

Combine 1 cup of the blueberries with 1 cup of the water and the sugar in a saucepan. Bring to a boil; then reduce the heat and simmer until the blueberries are tender. Strain the liquid and discard the blueberries. Bring the blueberry liquid to a boil. Mix the cornstarch with the remaining ¼ cup of water and stir it into the boiling liquid. Cook, stirring, until thick. Place the remaining blueberries in a large bowl and add the lemon juice. Pour the hot mixture over the blueberries and allow it to cool. Whip the cream until stiff, adding sugar to taste; then spoon into the pie shell. Pour the blueberry mixture over the whipped cream and chill for several hours. Makes one 9-inch pie.

CAROLANA CUSTARD

½ cup sugar
4 egg yolks, beaten
4 tbsp. cornstarch
pinch salt
1 tbsp. vanilla extract

2 cups non-dairy coffee
  creamer
3 cups boiling water
1½ cups confectioners' sugar

Combine the sugar, egg yolks, cornstarch, salt, vanilla, and coffee creamer in a saucepan and mix well. Stir in the boiling water slowly. Cook over medium heat for 3 to 5 minutes, stirring constantly until thickened. Hold the pan in cold water, and stir until cool. Pour the mixture into a bowl.

Place confectioners' sugar in a large skillet and stir over moderate heat until melted. Pour it over the custard and chill. Serves 6 to 8.

VIRGINIA DARE'S DONUTS

½ cup mashed potatoes
¾ cup sugar
1 egg
½ cup milk
2 cups flour

2½ tsp. baking powder
½ tsp. salt
½ tsp. nutmeg
oil for deep frying
powdered sugar

Combine the potatoes, sugar, egg, and milk in a bowl. Sift the flour, baking powder, salt, and nutmeg together; then stir them into the sugar mixture. Roll the dough out on a floured surface and cut with a doughnut cutter. Drop into deep, hot oil and fry until golden brown. Drain on absorbent paper and roll in powdered sugar. Makes 3 dozen.

TENNESSEE
The Volunteer State

From the Appalachian Mountains in the east to the Mississippi River in the west, stretches the long narrow state of Tennessee. The land was the home of Cherokee and Creek Indian tribes and derived its name from the Indian word *Tenassee,* the early capital of the Cherokee nation. Until the mid-1700s, the Indian tribes strongly resisted settlement by the white men—but settle the white men did.

In the middle 1700s, a hunter named Elisha Walker braved the winding country and left his name on the ridge that overlooks the Grand Canyon of Tennessee. Soon after, the English came from the east to trade with the French. Near the foot of the ridge, which is now known as Signal Mountain, they built a simple crude building which became known as "The French Store." It marked the first white settlement in the area. However, it was a Virginia pioneer, William Bean, who established the first permanent settlement along the Watauga River in 1769.

The Tennessee region was part of North Carolina at that time, but it was cut off from the mother colony by the boundless rugged mountain area. In 1772, the settlers formed their own government, the Watauga Association, and drew up the first written constitution to be adopted west of the Alleghenies. Shortly thereafter, Daniel Boone blazed what is known as the Wilderness Road, a trail winding from Virginia through the Blue Ridge and Allegheny mountains, making way for settlement in Tennessee.

The settlers managed to survive the perilous first years and, by 1796, Tennessee's western frontier was populated enough to seek admission into the Union. On June 1, 1796, Tennessee became the 16th state.

Tennessee has produced many famous leaders whose contributions helped to build our nation. Andrew Jackson, lawyer, congressman, judge, and general, was elected the seventh president of the United States in 1828. Two more Tennesseans were destined to become president—James Polk and Andrew Johnson, who was vice-president at the time of Lincoln's assassination. Yet another well-known congressman from the Volunteer State was the frontiersman Davey Crockett.

Tennessee earned the nickname the Volunteer State because of the number of volunteers it supplied in the Revolutionary War; and subsequently in the War of 1812 and the Mexican War—two and three times as many as any other state. It was destined to play just as important a role in the Civil War.

In the early 1800s, large farms developed in the Tennessee Valley and Central Basin area causing the number of slaves to greatly increase. By the time the war clouds began to gather, western and middle Tennesseans had sided with the Confederacy, while eastern Tennesseans remained strongly pro-Union. At the election on June 8, 1861, the referendum vote on secession was split. However, the secession vote carried, making Tennessee the last state to join the Confederacy—almost two months after the war actually began.

More Civil War battles were fought in Tennessee than any other state except Virginia. Some of the bloodiest fighting of the war took place on Tennessee soil: Shiloh, Murfreesboro, Chattanooga, Franklin, and the Battle of Nashville, which, in 1864, was the last aggressive action of the Confederate army.

When Johnny came marching home, he found a state battered and destitute. The Civil War was the bloodiest struggle the world had seen up to that time. It is said that the war stripped the South of its manhood. Over 700,000 soldiers and civilians perished in that four-year span, either from wounds or illness or both. But Tennessee, like the other Confederate states, remained undaunted.

After the war, Tennesee escaped the rule of carpetbaggers, who were politicians or adventurers from the North. The Carpetbaggers went south during the Reconstruction and took control of the state governments there. However, in Tennessee, voting was restricted to Negroes and whites who were loyal to the Union. This rule gave way to the organization of the first Ku Klux Klan (1866) in order to maintain white supremacy. Tennessee continued working and striving to become a better state, and its recovery was nothing short of miraculous. It entered the 20th century with renewed life and vigor.

With the outbreak of World War I, again living up to their nickname, nearly 100,000 Tennesseans volunteered for service. Perhaps the most outstanding volunteer in World War I was Tennessee's Sergeant Alvin C. York, the most decorated soldier of that war.

Following World War I, Tennessee continued an economic uphill climb. In 1933, Congress created the Tennessee Valley Authority

(TVA) to develop the natural resources of the basin. This opened new vistas to city residents, who by then, far exceeded the farm population. Tennessee gained additional prominence in World War II when Oak Ridge was established as the site of atomic energy projects.

There was another kind of energy that had been building up in Tennessee over the years—an energy generated by foot-stomping, fiddle-playing country music. It all started with the Grand Ole Opry radio broadcast and went on to include such celebrities as W.C. Handy, George Hay, Minnie Pearl, Hank Williams (Senior and Junior), Eddy Arnold, Dinah Shore, Dolly Parton, and "the King" himself—Elvis Presley. The music industry is to Tennessee what the cotton industry was to the Old South—the very life and breath of its people.

Tennessee today encompasses the best of both worlds—Old South tradition and New World technology. Hospitality is a word indigenous to the South; but in Tennessee, hospitality is more than a smile, a handshake, or a welcome. It's a genuine tradition of friendliness that is extended by both the mountain folk and the plantation owners. It's an invitation to dinner, an offer to spend the night, an earful of country music, and even a whirl across the floor to the "Tennessee Waltz."

TO PICKLE ONIONS

Choose all of a size and soak in boiling brine, when cold, drain them and put them in bottles, and fill up with hot distilled vinegar; if they are to be white, use white wine vinegar; if they are to be brown, use the best distilled vinegar, adding, in both cases, a little mace, ginger, and whole pepper.

TENNESSEE TURKEY SPREAD

2 cups cooked turkey, ground
1 small onion, minced
2 hard-cooked eggs, minced
½ cup ground almonds

salt and pepper
⅛ tsp. hot sauce
2 tbsp. mayonnaise
olives (optional)

In a mixing bowl, combine all ingredients except the mayonnaise. Add the mayonnaise to bind until a stiff paté is formed. Place in a bowl and decorate with olives, if desired. Chill and serve with assorted crackers. Serves 8 to 10.

AHA! APPLE SALAD

6 apples
1 banana, diced
½ cup raisins (soaked to plump)
½ cup chopped walnuts
¾ cup mayonnaise salad dressing

2 tbsp. orange juice
1 tbsp. honey
1 tsp. dried orange peel
½ tsp. ground celery seed
½ tsp. cinnamon

Peel and dice the apples. Add the banana, raisins, and nuts. Combine the remaining ingredients and pour over the fruit, stirring until coated. Serves 6.

LIL ABNER SALAD

1 tbsp. salt
2 medium carrots, sliced
   diagonally
2 medium cucumbers, sliced
   diagonally

1 cup fresh or drained canned
   pineapple chunks
lettuce
Daisy Mae Sesame Seed
   Dressing (see recipe)

Sprinkle salt over carrots and cucumbers; let stand for 5 minutes. Rinse vegetables thoroughly with ice water; then drain. Stir in the pineapple. Serve on a bed of lettuce and top with Daisy Mae Sesame Dressing (see recipe). Serves 4 to 6.

DAISY MAE SESAME DRESSING

½ cup salad oil
½ cup white wine vinegar
¼ cup sugar
¼ cup toasted sesame seeds

1 tsp. salt
1 tsp. ground ginger
½ cup minced green onion

Combine all ingredients, and store in refrigerator. Shake dressing well before using. Makes 1½ cups.

GRANDMAW'S GRIDDLECAKES

1½ cups sifted flour
2½ tsp. baking powder
¾ tsp. salt
3 tbsp. sugar

1 egg, well beaten
1 cup milk (about)
3 tbsp. butter or margarine,
   melted

Sift together the flour, baking powder, salt, and sugar. Combine the egg, milk, and melted butter or margarine. Pour the egg mixture into the flour mixture and stir just enough to moisten the dry ingredients. Do not beat. Drop by large tablespoons onto a hot griddle. When the edges begin to bubble, turn and brown the other side. Serve hot with additional butter (or margarine) and syrup, honey, or sweet preserves. Makes 1 to 1½ dozen pancakes.

Note: For thicker pancakes, decrease milk to ¾ cup; for thinner pancakes, increase milk to 1¼ cups.

OLE OPRY POTATO SOUP

1 qt. water	2 eggs, lightly beaten
1 tsp. salt, divided	½ cup milk (about)
3 medium-sized potatoes, peeled and sliced	½ cup butter
2 cups flour	1 cup milk
	1 small onion, chopped

In a 6-quart pot, bring the water and ½ teaspoon of salt to a boil. Add the potatoes; then cook until potatoes are done. With a potato masher or fork, mash the potatoes in the water.

Sift together the flour and ½ teaspoon salt in a medium mixing bowl. In a measuring cup, lightly beat the eggs, then fill with milk to one cup mark. Add the milk mixture to the flour mixture, making a soft dough.

Bring the potato water back to boiling. To this, add ½ cup butter and 1 cup milk. Bring to a simmering boil. Keep the soup simmering. Dip a teaspoon into the hot soup then dip up about ½ teaspoon of dough on the tip of spoon. Drop the dough into the simmering soup; stir and continue the process until all the dough has been used. Stir continuously. If it becomes too thick, add more milk. Cover and cook for about 20 minutes. Serve with chopped onions sprinkled on top. Serves 6.

MEM-FISH

1 3 to 4-lb. fish	2 tbsp. vinegar
salt to taste	¼ cup lemon juice
2 tbsp. chopped onion	3 tbsp. Worcestershire sauce
1 tbsp. vegetable shortening	2 tbsp. brown sugar
1 cup ketchup	dash pepper

Place the fish in a greased, shallow pan and sprinkle with salt. In the saucepan, sauté the onion in the shortening until tender. Add the remaining ingredients and simmer for 5 minutes. Pour the mixture over the fish. Bake at 425° for 35 to 40 minutes. Serves 6 to 8.

SMOKEE'S FISH PUFFS

1 cup flaked smoked white fish	1 cup shredded cheddar cheese
¼ cup chopped onion	1½ cups water
¼ cup chopped bell pepper	¾ cup butter or margarine
3 green onions, chopped	½ tsp. salt
1 tsp. dry mustard	1½ cups flour
1 tsp. Worcestershire sauce	6 eggs
2 tsp. red pepper sauce	

Preheat the oven to 400°. In a mixing bowl, combine the flaked fish, onions, and bell pepper. Add the mustard, Worcestershire sauce, red pepper sauce, and cheese. In a medium-sized saucepan, combine the water, butter (or margarine), and salt. Bring the mixture to a boil. Reduce the heat to low; then add the flour and stir vigorously until the mixture leaves the sides of the pan and forms a smooth ball.

Remove the saucepan from the heat and allow the mixture to cool slightly. Add the eggs, one at a time, beating with a wooden spoon after each addition. Beat until the batter is smooth. Add the fish mixture and stir well. Drop the batter by heaping teaspoons onto an ungreased baking sheet. Bake at 400° for 15 minutes. Reduce heat to 350° and bake an additional 10 minutes. Serve warm. Serves 6.

A GOBBLER CASSEROLE

2 cups cooked chopped
  turkey
1 10½-oz. can condensed
mushroom soup
2 tsp. finely chopped onion
1 cup finely chopped celery

½ tsp. pepper
½ tsp. salt
1 cup slivered almonds
1 tsp. lemon juice
¼ cup mayonnaise
½ cup pareve cracker crumbs

In a large mixing bowl, combine all ingredients, except the cracker crumbs, and mix well. Pour into a 1½-quart baking dish. Sprinkle the cracker crumbs over the top. Bake in a 375-degree oven for 25 minutes. Serves 4.

CORN BEEF: A-NU-WAY

2 tbsp. pareve margarine
¼ cup diced onion
2 tbsp. flour
1¼ cups finely chopped corn
  beef

1½ cups canned tomatoes,
  drained and chopped
1 recipe Shell pastry (see
  recipe)

Melt the pareve margarine, then add the onion and cook slowly until soft. Add the flour and stir until well blended. Add the corn beef and tomatoes. Bring to a boil, stirring constantly until thick and smooth. Let simmer 10 minutes. Fill the prepared Shell Pastry with the corn beef mixture. Fold the edges over and bake in a 425° oven for 20 minutes, or until the shells are browned. Serves 8.

POP'S CHICKEN POPOVER

3 tbsp. pareve margarine
1 tsp. dried sage leaves
¼ tsp. pepper
¼ cup flour
½ tsp. salt
1 3½-lb broiler-fryer, cut into
  serving pieces

3 large eggs
1 cup non-dairy creamer
½ cup water
1 tsp. baking powder
1 cup flour
½ tsp. salt
¼ cup chopped parsley

Preheat the oven to 400°. In a 15x9-inch baking pan, melt pareve margarine in the oven. Remove the baking pan from the oven.

On waxed paper, mix together the sage leaves, pepper, ¼ cup flour, and ½ teaspoon salt. Coat the chicken pieces with the flour mixture. Dip the chicken pieces, one at a time, into the melted margarine in the baking pan to coat both sides; then arrange the chicken, skin side up, in the pan. Bake for 30 minutes at 400 degrees.

In a large bowl, beat the eggs until frothy with a mixer at low speed. Beat in the non-dairy creamer and water until blended; then beat in the baking powder, 1 cup flour, and ½ teaspoon of salt until the batter is smooth. Stir in the parsley.

Pour the batter over the chicken in the baking pan. Bake for 25 minutes, or until the chicken is tender and the popover is puffed and golden brown. Serve immediately. Serves 4.

SHELL PASTRY

2 cups flour
1 tsp. baking powder
½ tsp. salt
4 level tbsp. vegetable
shortening

1 egg yolk, slightly beaten
⅓ cup non-dairy creamer

Sift the dry ingredients together. Add the shortening and mix thoroughly with a fork. Add the egg to the non-dairy creamer; then combine with the dry mix to form a soft dough. Roll out half of the dough to ⅛ inch thickness. Cut into square quarters. Fit each square into a muffin tin, fill with desired filling. Fold the edges of the pastry dough over into the center. Bake in a 425° oven for 20 minutes, or until the shells are nicely browned. Serves 8.

SCHLEPPER'S PIE
(Microwave)

1 lb. ground beef
1 medium onion
1 10-oz. pkg. frozen peas and
carrots, or cut green beans
1 10½-ounce can tomato
soup

1 tsp. Worcestershire sauce
½ tsp. salt
¼ tsp. basil
⅛ tsp. pepper
3 cups hot mashed potatoes

Crumble ground beef into a 2-quart casserole. Add the onion. Microwave on high for 4 to 6 minutes, or until the meat loses its pink color. Break up the meat and drain.

Microwave vegetables in their package on high for 2 to 3½ minutes, or until defrosted. Stir the tomato soup, Worcestershire sauce, salt, basil, and pepper into the ground beef mixture while microwaving vegetables. Spread evenly in the casserole dish. Sprinkle with the defrosted vegetables. Spoon mounds of mashed potatoes over the vegetables. Microwave for 5 to 7 minutes, or until the casserole is hot. Let stand 3 minutes before serving. Serves 4 to 6.

AMEN!! ACORN SQUASH
(Microwave and Conventional)

⅔ cup honey or maple syrup   2 acorn squash
¼ cup butter or margarine   ½ cup water (conventional
½ tsp. salt   method only)
1 tbsp. grated orange peel

MICROWAVE: Combine the honey (or maple syrup), butter, salt, and orange peel in a 2-cup glass measure. Cover tightly with plastic wrap, turning back one edge to vent. Microwave at 100% power for 4 to 5 minutes, or until the butter melts. Set aside.

Cut the squash in half lengthwise and scoop out the seeds. Trim off a thin slice from rounded sides so squash halves will sit firmly, cut side up. Arrange the squash, cut side down, in a glass baking dish. Cover tightly with plastic wrap, turning back one edge to vent. Microwave at 100% power for 5 minutes. Turn the cut side up. Pour the honey mixture in the squash halves and brush the cut surface of the squash with a little of the mixture. Cover, leaving a vent, and microwave at 100% power for 5 to 6 minutes, or until fork-tender, rotating the dish once during the cooking. Let stand, covered, for 5 minutes. Serves 4.

CONVENTIONAL: Preheat the oven to 350°. Cut the squash in half lengthwise and scoop out the seeds. Trim off a thin slice from the rounded sides, so the squash halves will sit firmly, cut side up. Place the squash, cut side down, in a large baking dish. Add ½ cup water and bake for 30 minutes. Melt the butter or margarine in a small saucepan. Stir in the honey, salt, and orange peel. Turn the squash halves cut side up. Pour the honey mixture into the squash halves and brush the cut surfaces of squash with the mixture. Bake for 25 to 30 minutes at 350° until fork-tender. Serves 4.

MIS' CLARA'S CUCUMBERS

3 cucumbers, 7 to 8 inches
  long
1 cup canned, flaked tuna or
  salmon
1 tsp. grated onion
¼ cup finely chopped celery

1 cup bread crumbs, divided
6 tbsp. mayonnaise
2 tbsp. lemon juice
½ tsp. salt
¼ tsp. pepper

Wash the cucumbers, cut them in half lengthwise and pare them. Boil for about 5 minutes until they are almost tender. Cut off a thin slice the length of each cucumber. Scoop out to make a shell about ½ inch thick. Sprinkle with salt. Chop the removed pulp.

Combine the tuna (or salmon), onion, celery, ½ cup of the bread crumbs, mayonnaise, lemon juice, and seasonings. Add the chopped cucumber pulp. Fill the cucumber shells with the fish mixture. Sprinkle with the remaining bread crumbs. Place in a shallow baking dish containing a little water. Bake in a 350° oven for about 30 minutes or until browned. Serves 6.

PARSNIPPY CASSEROLE

2 cups parsnips, cooked and
  mashed
1 cup applesauce
¼ cup brown sugar
1 tsp. salt

½ tsp. nutmeg
1 tbsp. lemon juice
¼ cup butter or margarine
½ cup bread crumbs

Arrange the parsnips and applesauce in layers in a greased 2-quart casserole. Sprinkle each layer with brown sugar, salt, nutmeg, lemon juice, and bits of butter or margarine. Top with bread crumbs. Bake in a 375-degree oven for 25 to 30 minutes, or until the top is browned. Serves 6.

POPEYE'S CHEEZY SPINACH

2 10-oz. pkg. frozen spinach
½ cup melted margarine
6 eggs lightly beaten
1 16-oz. container cottage
  cheese

1 10-oz. stick sharp cheddar
  cheese, cubed
½ cup grated cheddar cheese
1 tbsp. flour

Cook the spinach according to package directions and drain it. Mix the remaining ingredients together, adding the spinach last. Put the mixture in a greased, 2-quart pyrex dish. Bake in a 350° oven for 1 hour. Let set about 10 minutes before serving. Serves 4 to 6.

TURN-UP GREENS

2 bunches turnip greens
10 to 12 new potatoes

salt to taste
2 tbsp. margarine

Wash and drain the turnip greens. Place them in a large iron skillet with enough water to cover them. Scrub the new potatoes and place them on top of the greens. Add salt to taste. Cover the skillet and cook for 1 to 1½ hours until the potatoes are tender. Drain off any remaining water. Add the margarine and simmer until hot. Serves 6.

FUDGE CAKE IN A SKILLET

¼ cup vegetable shortening
4 oz. unsweetened chocolate
¼ cup milk
2 cups sugar
2 eggs
1 tsp. vanilla extract

2 tsp. baking powder
¼ tsp. salt
¼ tsp. baking soda
1⅞ cups flour
1 pint sour cream
powdered sugar

Melt the shortening and chocolate in a 10-inch cast iron frying pan. Remove from the heat and add the milk and sugar. Mix together the eggs and vanilla and add them to the pan. Add the baking powder, salt, baking soda, half of the flour, and half of the sour cream. Blend, then add the remaining flour and sour cream. Blend well. Bake in the frying pan at 350 degrees for 50 minutes. When cool, sprinkle with a little powdered sugar. Serves 10.

JACOB'S DREAMY DESSERT

½ cup soft vegetable
   shortening
1½ cups brown sugar, packed
1 cup flour
2 eggs, well beaten
1 tsp. vanilla

2 tbsp. flour
1 tsp. baking powder
½ tsp. salt
1 cup shredded coconut
1 cup chopped nuts

Mix together the shortening and ½ cup of the brown sugar. Stir in 1 cup of flour. Flatten the mixture into the bottom of an ungreased, oblong 13×9×2-inch pan. Bake in a 350-degree oven for 10 minutes.

Combine the eggs, 1 cup of brown sugar, and vanilla. Combine the 2 tablespoons of flour with the baking powder and salt. Mix egg mixture into the flour mixture. Stir in coconut and nuts. Pour over the baked layer. Return to the oven and bake for 25 minutes more. Cool and cut into bars. Makes 2½ dozen bars.

POLLYANNA'S POUND CAKE

2 sticks butter
2 cups sugar
6 eggs

3 cups flour
¼ tsp. salt
1 tbsp. vanilla extract

Cream the butter and sugar together in a mixing bowl. Add the eggs, one at a time, beating well after each addition. Mix the flour and salt together; then add them to the creamed mixture, a small amount at a time, beating well after each addition. Stir in the vanilla. Pour into a greased tube or loaf pan. Bake at 350 degrees for 1 hour, or until the cake tests done. Makes 1 cake; serves 8 to 10.

CHATTANOOGA CHEW CHEWS

1 cup sugar
1 cup light corn syrup
1 cup heavy cream
¼ tsp. salt

2 tbsp. butter
6 tbsp. evaporated milk
2 tsp. vanilla extract

Combine the sugar, corn syrup, cream, and salt in a heavy saucepan. Place over low heat and stir until the sugar is dissolved. Cook to 232° (soft ball stage), stirring occasionally.

Add the butter and evaporated milk alternately, a little at a time, to prevent scorching. Continue cooking to between 242° and 244° (firm ball stage), stirring constantly to prevent scorching. Test frequently in cold water after 240° to determine the consistency desired in the finished caramels.

Remove from heat and add the vanilla, stirring only enough to blend. Pour the mixture into a lightly greased pan to a depth of about ¾ inch. When the caramels are firm, cut with a sharp knife into ¾-inch squares. Wrap in waxed paper or plastic wrap. Makes about 1 pound.

SHAVUOT
The Feast of Weeks

About twenty centuries ago, long before there was a New World, the Jewish people made their exodus from Egypt. That event was the first uprising against slavery to be recorded in history. When the slaves broke the shackles of bondage, they naturally turned their faces toward the land of their ancestors. It was the Promised Land, the land that God set aside for his chosen people.

After a long and gruelling journey, which lasted forty years, and a myriad of trials, tribulations, and much grumbling, the Jewish people were welded into a nation. At the foot of Mt. Sinai, the people gathered. Amid awe-inspiring solemnity, Moses, their leader, descended carrying the Ten Commandments that God gave to the Children of Israel. These, together with the laws of the Torah, were the fundamental laws accepted by them to govern their lives. The Ten Commandments have since become the possession of all mankind. This brief charter has proven to be not only the foundation of Judaism, but also the foundation upon which all modern civilization is based. The Jewish festival of Shavuot (or Feast of Weeks) commemorates this phenomenon.

Shavuot, however, began as an agricultural festival when most of our Jewish ancestors in ancient Palestine were farmers. Shavuot marked the end of the spring grain harvest, for which the people gave thanks and rejoiced. The one-day holiday (two days in the Diaspora) falls on the 6th day of the Hebrew month of Sivan, seven weeks after Passover (thus the name the "Feast of Weeks").

Shavuot today is a twofold holiday. In prayers, ceremonies, and customs, both the Torah (the scroll containing the Five Books of Moses) and the agricultural meaning of the festival are abundantly reflected. The meaning of Shavuot can be easily remembered by keeping in mind the name of the holiday. Shavuot stands for the seven weeks of harvest. As in ancient times, the Jews in Israel today engage in gathering their grain at this time of the year. At the end of the harvest, they celebrate and remember the Temple with appropriate ceremonies and programs. Shavuot also stands for the giving of the Law and the ideal of Jewish learning.

The customs of Shavuot are as revealing as its name. Reading the Ten Commandments and the Book of Ruth tells of both Torah and land. Eating dairy dishes, decorating homes, synagogues, and centers with flowers and greenery are concrete symbols of both learning and soil. The new ceremonies, called Confirmation in our own country, prove to us that the message of Shavuot is just as important in our own times as it was in the past.

After the Synagogue services, come and celebrate with us. Rejoice with delicious kugels, a favorite dairy dish, and indulge in scrumptuous desserts. Be merry! Dance the Hora and sing Hava Nagila, for the song says it all: "Come let us Rejoice."

AN EASY RECEIPT FOR A CHARLOTTE RUSSE.

Trim straitly about six ounces of savoy biscuits, so that they may fit closely to each other; line the bottom and sides of a plain mould with them, then fill it with a fine cream made in the following manner: put into a stewpan three ounces of ratafias, six of sugar, the grated rind of half an orange, the same quantity of the rind of a lemon, a small piece of cinnamon, a wine glass full of good maraschino, or fine noyeau, one pint of cream, and the well beaten yolks of six eggs; stir this mixture for a few minutes over a stove fire, and then strain it, add half a pint more cream whipped, and one ounce of dissolved isinglass. Mix the whole well together, and set it in a basin imbedded in rough ice; when it has remained a short time in the ice, fill the mould with it, and then place the mould in ice, or in a cool place, till ready to serve.

MOSES MARINATED HERRING

¼ cup mayonnaise
½ pint sour cream
1 tsp. celery seed
1 tsp. sugar
½ lemon, juice only
½ green bell pepper, chopped

½ red bell pepper, chopped
4 green onions, sliced
1 sweet onion, sliced thin
1 16-oz. jar herring in wine
  sauce, well drained

In a bowl, combine the mayonnaise, sour cream, celery seed, sugar, and lemon juice. Stir in the vegetables and herring. Marinate in a covered jar or glass bowl in the refrigerator for at least 24 hours. Serves 4.

JUST PLAIN CHEESE BLINTZES

2 eggs, beaten
½ cup sifted flour
¾ cup milk
1 tbsp. butter, melted
salt
butter for frying

1 lb. cream cheese
1 egg yolk
2 tbsp. sugar
dash cinnamon (or a few
    drops of vanilla)

Make a thin batter by combining the two eggs with the flour and milk alternately while beating with a fork. Work in the melted butter and a pinch of salt until smooth. In a separate bowl, combine the cream cheese, egg yolk, sugar, a pinch of salt, and cinnamon with a fork until soft enough to spread.

Heat a heavy frying pan and butter well. Pour in a thin stream of batter, starting at the center and tilting the pan to spread the mixture evenly across the bottom. Reduce the heat as soon as you begin pouring on the batter to make a well-baked layer for the first blintze. When the underside is lightly browned, turn out on a thick kitchen towel, browned side up. Start the second blintze layer, buttering the pan before pouring in batter.

While each blintze is baking on the frying pan, spread the browned side that was just turned out with the filling. Spread evenly; then roll up each blintze, tucking in the ends. When all are filled and rolled up, cut them in two and fry them in butter until nicely browned on both sides. Serve with sour cream, preserves, or sugar and cinnamon. Makes 12 blintzes.

BLESSED BE! BUTTERMILK BORSCHT

4 cups boiling water
3½ tsp. salt
1 medium-sized onion, peeled
1 clove garlic, peeled
2 bunches beets, washed, peeled, and coarsely shredded

5 tbsp. sugar
2 tbsp. lemon juice
2 eggs, beaten
2 cups buttermilk
12 cooked small white potatoes, cold
3 tsp. finely chopped fresh dill

To the boiling water, add the salt, whole onion, garlic, beets, sugar, and lemon juice. Cover and simmer for 45 minutes, or until the onion is soft. Remove the onion and garlic. Cool the beet mixture slightly. Add the beaten eggs gradually, stirring vigorously. Chill. Add the buttermilk; mix well. Serve cold, garnished with 2 whole potatoes sprinkled with ½ teaspoonful of dill. Serves 6.

APPLE ANNIE'S KUGEL

4 tbsp. margarine
½ lb. fine noodles, cooked and drained
3 eggs
¼ cup sugar

1 tsp. cinnamon
½ cup bread crumbs, divided
3 cups sweetened applesauce, fresh or canned

Melt the margarine in a skillet; then sauté the noodles until they are browned. Set aside.

Beat together the eggs, sugar, cinnamon, and ¼ cup of the bread crumbs. Add the browned noodles and mix well. In a greased, 2-quart baking pan, arrange alternate layers of the noodle mixture and the applesauce, starting and ending with the noodles. Sprinkle the remaining bread crumbs on top; then bake at 350 degrees for 30 minutes. Serves 8.

SIGH-NIGH SALMON CASSEROLE

4 oz. extra broad noodles	2 eggs, beaten
¼ cup butter or margarine	1 8-oz. can salmon, drained
¼ cup flour	2 tbsp. minced parsley
½ tsp. salt	1 cup cooked peas
½ tsp. onion powder	¼ cup diced celery
2 cups milk	2 tsp. lemon juice

Cook noodles in boiling salted water until tender (about 5 minutes). Drain and rinse. Melt the butter in the top half of a double boiler. Stir in the flour and salt. Add the milk and cook until thickened, stirring constantly. Pour 1 cup of this white sauce over the beaten eggs, stirring until well blended. Fold in the noodles, salmon, and parsley. Place in 1½-quart casserole. Set the casserole dish in a shallow pan of water, then bake at 350 degrees for about 40 minutes.

While salmon-noodle mixture is baking, fold the peas, celery, and lemon juice into the remaining white sauce in the double boiler. Keep warm over hot water. Unmold salmon-noodle mixture and top with the creamed vegetables. Serves 4.

FESTIVE FISH KUGEL

½ cup butter	1½ tsp. salt
2 onions, sliced	½ tsp. pepper
3 potatoes, peeled and sliced	2 eggs
3 cups cooked flaked fish	1½ cups heavy cream

Preheat the oven to 350°. Melt the butter in a skillet; then brown the onions. Set alternate layers of potatoes, fish, and onions in a buttered baking dish, ending with potatoes on top. Sprinkle the potatoes with salt and pepper. Beat the eggs with the cream; then pour over contents of baking dish. Bake for 45 minutes at 350 degrees until firm. Serves 6.

THE CHOSEN CHEESE KUGEL

1 8-oz. pkg. cream cheese, softened
1 cup cottage cheese
2 eggs, beaten
½ tsp. salt
dash pepper
3 cups (6 ounces) noodles, cooked and drained
2 tbsp. dry bread crumbs

Combine the cream cheese, cottage cheese, eggs, salt, and pepper. Mix until well blended. Add the noodles and mix lightly. Sprinkle a greased 4½-cup ring mold with bread crumbs; then spoon the noodle mixture into the mold. Bake at 375° for 30 minutes. Invert onto a serving plate. Serves 6 to 8.

EGGPLANT KUGEL WITH A KICK

1 large eggplant (about 2 lb.)
½ tsp. salt
3 tbsp. olive oil
1 onion, chopped
1 sweet green pepper, chopped
2 tbsp. chopped fresh basil
2 eggs, slightly beaten
1 matzoh cracker, crumbled
½ tsp. salt
½ tsp. pepper
1 tbsp. margarine

Peel the eggplant; then cut it into 2-inch cubes. In medium-size saucepan, simmer in salted water to cover for 20 minutes or until tender. Drain, then mash in a large bowl.

Heat the olive oil in a medium-sized skillet over medium heat. Add the onion and green pepper and cook until tender (about 8 minutes). Add the vegetables to the mashed eggplant in the bowl. Stir in the basil, eggs, matzoh, salt, and pepper. Pour into a greased 1½-quart casserole. Dot with margarine.

Bake in a 350-degree oven for 35 minutes. Serves 8.

KREPLACH TO KVELL

2 eggs, beaten
½ cup water
½ tsp. salt
2 to 2¼ cups flour
1 8-oz. pkg. cream cheese,
  softened

1 egg, beaten
2 tbsp. finely chopped onions
2 tbsp. chopped parsley
2 tbsp. dry bread crumbs
margarine for frying

Combine two beaten eggs with the water. Add the salt and enough of the flour to form a soft dough. On a lightly floured surface, knead the dough until smooth and elastic. Cover and let stand for 10 minutes. Divide the dough in half. On a lightly floured surface, roll each half to ⅛-inch thickness; then cut into 3-inch squares.

Combine the cream cheese and the one beaten egg, mixing until well blended. Add the onion, parsley, and crumbs; then mix well. Place a rounded teaspoonful of the cream cheese mixture onto each dough square. Fold the dough to form triangles; then press the edges to seal. Cook, a few at a time, in boiling salted water for 3 to 4 minutes or until the kreplach float; then drain. Fry in margarine until lightly browned. Makes about 2 dozen.

KREAMY POTATO KUGEL

1 8-oz. pkg. cream cheese,
  softened
3 eggs, beaten
¼ cup margarine, melted
¼ cup flour

½ tsp. baking powder
½ tsp. salt
3 cups shredded peeled
  potatoes, drained
¼ cup chopped onion

Combine the cream cheese, eggs, and margarine, mixing until well blended. Add the combined flour, baking powder, and salt; then mix well. Stir in the potatoes and onions. Pour the mixture into a well-greased, 10x6-inch baking dish. Bake at 350 degrees for 50 minutes. Serves 6.

KUGEL MIT ROZHINKES

1 8-oz. pkg. cream cheese, softened
¼ cup margarine, melted
4 eggs, beaten
½ cup milk
¼ cup sugar

½ tsp. salt
4 cups (8 oz.) narrow noodles, cooked and drained
½ cup raisins

Combine the cream cheese and margarine, mixing until well blended. Blend in the eggs, milk, sugar, and salt. Add the noodles and raisins; mix well. Pour the mixture into a 12x8-inch baking dish. Bake at 375 degrees for 30 minutes or until set. Serves 6 to 8.

NU AWLINS KUGEL

1 8-oz. pkg. ½-inch wide noodles
1 8-oz. pkg. cream cheese, softened
1 cup sour cream
¼ lb. unsalted butter, melted and cooled

3 large eggs
¼ cup sugar
1 tsp. vanilla extract
pinch salt
4 pecan pralines, finely crumbled

Cook the noodles according to the package instructions; then drain well.

Meanwhile, in a large bowl, beat together the cream cheese, sour cream, butter, eggs, sugar, vanilla, and salt until the mixture is fairly smooth. Stir in the drained noodles.

Pour the mixture into a buttered, two-quart casserole dish measuring 8x8x2½ inches. Bake in a preheated 350-degree oven until the top begins to brown (about 35 minutes). Sprinkle the praline pieces evenly over the top and continue baking until they melt and bubble (about 12 minutes). Cut the kugel into nine squares and serve while still warm. Serves 6 to 8.

A SHAVUOT POTATO SHISSEL
(Microwave and Conventional)

1 8-oz. pkg. cream cheese,
cubed
1 cup milk (1¼ cups for
Microwave method)
½ tsp. salt

¼ tsp. pepper
¾ cup shredded carrots
¼ cup green onion slices
4 cups thin peeled potato
slices

MICROWAVE: In a 2-quart casserole, microwave the cream cheese, 1¼ cups of milk, salt, and pepper on high for 1½ to 2 minutes, or until the sauce is smooth when stirred. Stir in the carrots and onions. Add the potatoes; mix lightly. Cover and microwave on high for 20 to 22 minutes, or until the potatoes are tender. Stir every 5 minutes. Serves 6.

CONVENTIONAL: Combine the cream cheese, 1 cup of milk, salt, and pepper in a saucepan. Stir over low heat until smooth. Stir in the carrots and onions. Add the potatoes and mix lightly. Spoon into a 10x6-inch baking dish; then cover with foil. Bake at 350 degrees for 55 minutes. Uncover and continue baking for 15 minutes, or until the potatoes are tender. Serves 6.

MAX'S RONI AND CHEESE

1 8-oz. pkg. elbow macaroni
2 cups shredded sharp
cheddar cheese
1¾ cups milk

3 eggs
1 tsp. salt
1 tsp. dry mustard

Preheat the oven to 350°. Prepare the elbow macaroni according to the package directions. Drain. To the hot macaroni, in the same saucepan, add the remaining ingredients except ½ cup of the cheese. Mix well. Cook, stirring, over medium heat for 3 to 5 minutes until the cheese melts. Place in a greased, 1½-quart baking dish. Top with remaining cheese. Bake for 20 to 25 minutes at 350 degrees until bubbly. Serves 6 to 8.

SHEBA'S SPINACH PIE

1 qt. chopped fresh spinach
½ cup chopped onion
1 8-oz. pkg. cream cheese,
 softened
¾ cup ricotta cheese
½ tsp. dried crushed basil

½ tsp. dried crushed oregano
¼ tsp. salt
⅛ tsp. garlic powder
⅛ tsp. pepper
¾ cup chopped tomato
2 tbsp. parmesan cheese

Preheat the oven to 350 degrees. Place the spinach and onions in a small saucepan. Cover and cook for about 5 minutes, or until tender. In a small mixing bowl, beat the cream cheese, ricotta cheese, and seasonings with an electric mixer at medium speed until well blended. Stir in the spinach mixture; then spread into a 9-inch pie pan. Bake for 15 to 20 minutes or until thoroughly heated. Top with chopped tomato and parmesan cheese. Serves 8.

TRADITIONAL POTATO KUGEL

3 eggs, separated
8 large potatoes, peeled,
 grated, and drained
2 large onions, grated
salt and pepper to taste

1 cup fine bread crumbs
pinch baking powder
⅓ cup schmaltz or vegetable
 oil

Preheat the oven to 350 degrees. Beat the egg whites until they are stiff. In a large bowl, combine all ingredients except the egg whites and schmaltz. Mix well. Fold in the egg whites and mix again. Pour the mixture into a greased baking pan. Bake at 350 degrees for 1 hour, or until the edges and top are brown and crisp. Slice in the pan. Serves 10.

UPSIDE DOWN "SPIKED" KUGEL

1 16-oz. pkg. fine noodles
3 eggs, well beaten
1 cup sugar
1 tsp. salt
1 tsp. cinnamon
⅓ cup vegetable oil
1 cup golden raisins

¼ cup Sabra liqueur
6 tbsp. butter or margarine
¾ cup brown sugar
4 slices canned pineapple
maraschino cherries
pecan or walnut halves

Cook the noodles according to the package directions. Drain well. Combine the eggs, sugar, salt, cinnamon, vegetable oil, raisins, and liqueur; mix well. Toss with noodles. Melt the butter in a deep, 10-inch pan or ring mold, greasing the sides lightly. Sprinkle the brown sugar evenly over the melted butter in the bottom of the pan. Arrange pineapple, cherries, and nuts over the sugar. Pour the noodle mixture over the fruit. Bake in a 350° oven for 1 hour. Leave in the pan for 5 minutes after removing from oven; then unmold onto a large serving platter. Serves 8.

YUMMY YAM KUGEL

2 cups shredded raw sweet
  potatoes
1 cup shredded apple
¾ cup margarine, melted
¾ cup packed brown sugar
1 cup flour

1 tsp. baking soda
½ tsp. cinnamon
½ tsp. ground nutmeg
½ tsp. salt
½ cup raisins
½ cup chopped nuts

Combine the sweet potatoes, apples, margarine, and sugar; mix well. Combine the dry ingredients; then add them to sweet potato mixture, mixing just until moistened. Fold in the raisins and nuts. Pour into 10x6-inch baking dish. Cover with foil. Bake at 350 degrees for 1 hour. Uncover, continue baking for 10 minutes. Serves 6 to 8.

YONKEL DOODLE NOODLE

8 oz. broad noodles
3 tbsp. pareve margarine
3 eggs
1 tsp. cinnamon

¼ tsp. nutmeg
¾ cup sugar
⅛ tsp. salt
½ cup seedless raisins

Boil the noodles according to the directions on the package. Drain and rinse in cold water. Separate the eggs. Add the margarine, well-beaten egg yolks, cinnamon, nutmeg, sugar, salt, and raisins to the noodles. Mix well. Fold in stiffly beaten egg whites. Pour into a greased, oblong baking dish and bake at 350 degrees for about 45 minutes, until nicely brown. Cut into squares. Serves 6.

CHEESECAKE FOR MISHPOCHEH

1 cup graham cracker crumbs
3 tbsp. sugar
3 tbsp. butter or margarine, melted
2 8-oz. pkg. cream cheese, softened
¾ cup sugar

⅓ cup cocoa
1 tsp. vanilla
2 eggs
1 cup sour cream
2 tbsp. sugar
1 tsp. vanilla

Combine the graham cracker crumbs, 3 tablespoons of sugar, and butter. Press onto the bottom of a 9-inch springform pan. Bake at 325 degrees for 10 minutes.

Combine the cream cheese, ¾ cup sugar, cocoa, and vanilla. Mix at medium speed with an electric mixer until well blended. Add the eggs, one at a time, mixing well after each addition. Pour the mixture over the crust. Bake at 375 degrees for 30 minutes.

Combine the sour cream, 2 tablespoons of sugar, and 1 teaspoon of vanilla. Mix well. Carefully spread over the cheesecake. Bake at 425 degrees for 10 minutes. Loosen the cake from the rim of the pan. Cool before removing the rim of the pan. Chill before serving. Serves 10 to 12.

COMMAND-MINT PIE

1 cup graham cracker crumbs
2 tbsp. powdered sugar
3 tbsp. butter or margarine,
  melted
½ cup butter
1 cup powdered sugar

2 squares semi-sweet
  chocolate, melted
2 eggs
¼ tsp. peppermint extract
1 tsp. vanilla extract

Combine the crumbs, 2 tablespoons powdered sugar, and 3 tablespoons of butter. Press into an 8-inch pie plate and bake at 325 degrees for 5 minutes. Chill.

Cream the ½ cup of butter and 1 cup of powdered sugar until fluffy. Slowly add the melted chocolate. Add the eggs, one at a time, beating well after each addition. Add the peppermint and vanilla. Pour into pie shell. Chill for 6 hours before serving. Makes one 8-inch pie.

Topping (Optional)

sweetened whipped cream
¼ cup toasted, slivered
  almonds

1 square semi-sweet
  chocolate, grated

Just before serving, top pie with whipped cream. Garnish with almonds and grated chocolate. Makes enough topping for one 8-inch pie.

SUCCOTH
Feast of Booths

For thousands of years, harvest festivals have been celebrated in many lands. In the United States and in Canada, we observe a Thanksgiving holiday which probably grew out of the harvest-home celebrations of England. In the United States, Thanksgiving has been celebrated since the second winter that the Plymouth colonists spent in the New World. From 1622 to the present, one day a year has been set aside for people to give thanks with prayer and feasting.

The custom of harvest festivals has been celebrated among the Jewish people since the Exodus from Egypt. The holiday of Succoth (the Feast of Booths) could be called the Jewish Thanksgiving. Many comparisons have been made between Succoth and Thanksgiving. However, there is one major difference: the Jewish people rejoice for eight days with a special ninth day called Simchat Torah immediately following. During Succoth, thanks are given for many things: the fall harvest, the momentous forty-year journey to the Promised Land, the yearly completion and the immediate new beginning of the reading of the Torah during Simchat Torah (showing that the reading of Torah has neither beginning nor end). Additionally, the holiday recalls the temporary tabernacles, or booths, in which the Jews lived while in the desert. God gave the Jewish people booths in which to dwell in the desert as a sign of His protectiveness.

During their forty years of wandering, the Jewish people hastily set up temporary booths in which to dwell. Today, the booths are re-created in Jewish homes throughout the world. The Succah (booth) is intended to look temporary. It is constructed outdoors and roofed with loose branches so the stars can be seen from the inside. The interior is decorated with fruits and flowers, another reminder of the fall harvest. Because Succoth is a family-oriented holiday, the children join with the family to adorn the Succah. During the eight-day festival, many families have all their meals in the Succah.

One might say that it is a divine commandment to eat magnificently during these eight days of Succoth. There are no limitations or restrictions on what foods can or cannot be prepared. Therefore, Succoth becomes a cook's delight. It is an opportune time to be creative, to serve abundantly, and enjoy the *nachas* of being with *mishpocheh* (the extended family).

Everything seems to take on a special holiday taste at Succoth meals. Songs are sung between courses. The ambiance could not be more festive! We look at the faces of our children and we bless them and pray for them. They are our hope and future. It is appropriate to close the holiday with the singing of *Hatikva*, the Jewish National Anthem, for appropriately Hatikva literally means "The Hope."

COMPOTE OF APPLES

1 Dozen Apples   **½ Cup of Water**
2 Cups of Sugar

Pare the apples, cut them in quarters, cut out the cores, and place them several times to drain the juice. Boil six apples, 2 cups of sugar and half a cup of water and add the finely cut peel of a lemon, together with the lemon juice. When they are well blanched, take them out without letting them cook too much, and place them in a dish. They must be soft, but not pithy. Put the other apples that you have cut into quarters into the syrup, let them boil to a jelly in the juice. Put all together in a nice dish. Sprinkle with a little grated nutmeg and powdered sugar. This is excellent.

To make a compote of whole apples, first remove the core of each apple its whole length, by inserting a long tin cutter at one end, and then at the other end, and with the finger force the core out. In this way you will not split the apples. Finish as in the above recipe.

EGGS-ZIT SPREAD

6 hard-boiled eggs   **2 tbsp. smaltz (chicken fat)**
½ cup minced onions   **at room temperature (or**
salt to taste   **mayonnaise)**
pepper to taste

Chop the eggs and onions together until well blended. Season to taste with the salt and pepper. Add fat or mayonnaise to bind the mixture together. Serve as a salad on a bed of lettuce, as a spread, or as a filling for sandwiches. Serves 6 for salads or sandwiches, or 12 as a spread.

KIBBUTZ CUCUMBER SALAD

2 heads lettuce, broken into
small pieces
4 tomatoes, skinned and
quartered
1 cucumber, peeled, scored,
and sliced thin

8 or 10 radishes, sliced thin
½ green pepper, shredded
1 tsp. sugar
salt and pepper to taste
salad dressing of your choice

Put the vegetables in a large bowl, add the seasonings, and pour the salad dressing over all. Toss lightly until well mixed. Serves 6 to 8.

BALABATISH BARLEY SOUP

1 oz. dried mushrooms
2 lb. soup meat (top rib or
flanken)
2 qt. water
2 tsp. salt
½ cup pearl barley

1 onion, diced
2 carrots, peeled and diced
2 sprigs parsley
1 sprig dill
1 bay leaf
pepper to taste

Wash and soak the mushrooms according to the directions on the package. Place the meat in the salted water and bring to a boil. Reduce the heat and simmer for about 45 minutes. Skim.

Wash and drain the barley. Add the barley, drained mushrooms, onion, carrots, and seasonings. Simmer for about 1½ hours, or until the meat and vegetables are tender. Remove the parsley, dill, and bay leaf before serving. Serves 6.

CURE ALL CHICKEN SOUP

5- to 6-lb. chicken, disjointed
2 lb. necks, wings, backs and
  gizzards
5 qt. water
2 stalks celery with leaves,
  cut in 2-inch pieces
2 carrots, peeled and cut in
  2-inch pieces

1 large onion, quartered
1 tbsp. salt
pinch white pepper
1 bay leaf
2 sprigs parsley
4 sprigs fresh dill

In a large soup pot, cover the chicken and parts with water. Bring to a rapid boil and skim carefully. Lower the flame and simmer for 2 hours. Skim again, if necessary. Add the vegetables and seasonings. Simmer for 2 more hours. Strain through a fine strainer or 2 layers of cheesecloth. (If you desire a clear broth, do not squeeze the cooked vegetables through the final straining). Chill the broth overnight. Remove the congealed layer of fat and reheat. Serves 8 to 10.

FISH FROM THE JAWS

2 tbsp. butter or margarine
¼ cup chopped green pepper
½ cup chopped onion
½ tsp. salt
⅛ tsp. pepper
¼ tsp thyme

1 10½-oz. can condensed
  tomato soup
1 cup milk
1 1-lb. jar gefilte fish, drained
2 cups cooked rice
paprika

Sauté the onion and green pepper in butter until tender but not brown. Add the salt, pepper, thyme, tomato soup, and milk. Mix with rice. Pour the mixture into a greased, 1½-quart baking dish. Arrange the fish on top and press them into the rice mixture. Sprinkle with paprika. Bake in a 350-degree oven for 30 minutes. Serves 4.

BLUSHING DUCK

1 4½ to 5½-lb duckling,
  prepared and disjointed
2 cloves garlic
3 tbsp. flour
⅛ tsp. celery salt
⅛ tsp. onion powder
⅛ tsp. paprika

3 tbsp. schmaltz (chicken fat)
  or other vegetable
  shortening
2 cups stewed fresh
  cranberries, (or 1 16-oz.
  can whole cranberry sauce)

Rub each piece of duck with garlic. Combine the flour, celery salt, onion powder, and paprika. Roll each piece of duck in the flour mixture until well coated. Melt the fat in the bottom of a roasting pan; then add the duck pieces. Top with cranberry sauce, cover, and bake in a 325-degree oven for 45 to 50 minutes per pound (about 3 to 3½ hours), until the meat is fork-tender. Serves 5 to 6.

FRUIT AND FOWL

2 tbsp. flour
½ tsp. salt
½ tsp. pepper
1 3 to 4-lb. broiler-fryer, cut
  into serving pieces
¼ cup peanut oil
½ cup white wine

⅓ cup orange juice
2 tbsp. honey
1 tbsp. chopped parsley
2 tbsp. slivered orange peel
1 cup seedless white grapes,
  halved

Combine the flour, salt, and ¼ teaspoon of the pepper; then dust chicken pieces lightly. In a large skillet, brown the chicken in the peanut oil. Add the wine, orange juice, honey, parsley, and remaining ¼ teaspoon of pepper. Cover and simmer over low heat for 30 minutes. Stir occasionally. Add orange peel. Continue cooking until tender (10 to 15 minutes).

Remove the chicken to a serving platter. Add the grapes to the gravy and cook, stirring constantly, for 2 minutes. Pour over the chicken. Garnish with additional grapes and orange slices if desired. Serves 4 to 5.

A SIMCHA STEAK

2 tbsp. flour
⅛ tsp. salt
⅛ tsp. pepper
2-lb. shoulder steak
3 tbsp. vegetable oil

1 onion, chopped
1 tsp. Kosher steak sauce
1 20-oz. can tomatoes
1 green pepper, sliced in
  rings

Combine the flour, salt, and pepper. Pound the flour mixture into the meat on both sides. Heat the oil in a large, heavy skillet. Brown the meat on both sides. Add the remaining ingredients, except for the green pepper, and simmer for 2½ to 3 hours or until tender.

Add the green pepper rings and cook for 10 minutes more. Remove the meat to a platter and strain the gravy. Return the meat and gravy to the skillet for a few minutes until hot enough to serve. Serves 4.

A STEW NOT TO STEW OVER
(Microwave)

2 lb. beef stew meat, cut into
  1-inch cubes
2 cups water
2 6-oz. cans tomato paste
1 1.2-oz. pkg. dry onion
  soup mix
¼ tsp. garlic powder

¼ tsp. pepper
2 medium potatoes, peeled
  and cut into 1-inch cubes
2 medium carrots, peeled and
  sliced
1 12-oz. can yellow kernel
  corn

In a 3-quart casserole, combine the meat, water, tomato paste, onion soup mix, garlic powder, and pepper. Stir well and cover. Microwave on medium for 60 minutes, stirring every 20 minutes. Add the potatoes and carrots. Microwave on medium for 15 to 20 minutes more, until the meat is tender. Add the corn, stirring well. Microwave on high for 5 to 10 minutes, until the vegetables are tender. Stir well before serving. Serves 8 to 10.

CABBAGE—HOW SWEET IT IS!
(Microwave)

1 onion
1 tart apple
2 tbsp. pareve margarine
3 cups shredded red cabbage
(about ¾ lb.)
2 tbsp. wine vinegar

1 tbsp. brown sugar
1 tbsp. golden raisins
⅛ tsp. ground allspice
½ tsp. salt
pepper to taste

Chop the onion fine. Peel the apple and cut it into ½-inch cubes. Microwave the margarine on high, uncovered in a microwavable casserole, until melted. Stir in the onions; then cover and cook for 2 minutes on high. Add the shredded cabbage, apple, vinegar, sugar, raisins, allspice, and about ½ teaspoon of salt. Cover and microwave on high for about 14 minutes, stirring every 2 minutes, until tender. Let stand 2 minutes. Add pepper to taste. Serves 4.

CUZINEE'S CAULIFLOWER

1 10½-ounce can condensed
mushroom soup
1 large whole cauliflower,
cooked

¼ cup Kosher pareve
seasoned bread crumbs
1 tablespoon parmesan
cheese (optional)

Heat the condensed mushroom soup. Do not thin the soup. Place the whole cooked cauliflower in a casserole. Pour the hot mushroom soup over the cauliflower. Sprinkle generously with seasoned bread crumbs. If desired, sprinkle parmesan cheese over the top. Place in a preheated 400° oven for 15 minutes. Serves 4 to 6.

A GAHNTZE TZIMMES

1 17-oz. can sweet potatoes
1 20-oz. can sweetened
  apple slices
½ cup raisins
¼ cup chopped walnuts
⅓ cup honey

¼ cup peanut oil
2 tbsp. grated orange rind
½ tsp. salt
⅛ tsp. cinnamon
⅛ tsp. ginger

Place alternate layers of sweet potatoes, apple slices, raisins, and chopped walnuts in a lightly oiled, 1½-quart casserole. Combine the honey, peanut oil, orange rind, salt, cinnamon, and ginger; then pour the mixture over the sweet potatoes. Bake, uncovered, at 350 degrees for about 1 hour. Serves 6 to 8.

MISH-MOSH KASHA

1 cup medium roasted
  buckwheat kernels
1 egg, beaten
1½ cups water
1½ cups shredded zucchini

1 cup shredded carrots
¼ cup chopped onion
½ cup margarine, melted
dash pepper
chopped parsley

Combine the buckwheat kernels and egg; then cook, stirring constantly, over low heat until the grains are dry and separated. Add the water, vegetables, margarine, and pepper; mix well. Cover and simmer for 10 minutes. Sprinkle with parsley. Serves 6 to 8.

UNPRETENTIOUS SPICED POTATOES

2½ cups water
4 cups peeled and diced raw
  potatoes
3 cups peeled and diced
  apples

¼ cup chopped onion
2 tbsp. peanut oil
1 tbsp. salt
1 tbsp. potato starch
½ tsp. cinnamon

Measure the water and pour into a saucepan. Add the diced potatoes, apples, and chopped onion. Bring to a boil; then cover the pan and simmer until the potatoes are tender. Drain and reserve ¾ cup of the hot liquid.

Combine the peanut oil, salt, potato starch, and cinnamon. Add the mixture to the reserved hot potato liquid. Cook over medium heat until the mixture is thickened. Fold into the cooked potatoes and apples and serve hot. Serves 6 to 8.

ADAM'S APPLES

⅓ cup sugar
1 tsp. nutmeg
½ tsp. cinnamon

⅛ tsp. salt
4 large cooking apples
5 tbsp. butter or margarine

Mix together the sugar, nutmeg, cinnamon, and salt. Wash, core, and slice the apples into ½-inch slices. Heat the butter or margarine in a frying pan. Add the apple rings and ½ of the sugar mixture to the pan. Cook for about 3 minutes. Turn, then sprinkle with the remainder of the sugar mixture. Continue cooking until the apples are almost transparent. Serve hot. Serves 6.

ALEF BAZE APPLES
(Microwave)

4 medium apples (about 1 lb.)
4 tsp. sugar
4 tbsp. Sabra liqueur

2½ tbsp. chopped pecans
4 tsp. chopped raisins
½ tsp. cinnamon

Remove the cores from the apples with a melon baller, leaving a ½-inch thick shell. Do not pierce the bottoms. Remove ½ inch of the peel from top of each apple. Put 1 teaspoon of sugar in each apple. Pour 1 tablespoon of liqueur over the sugar in each apple. Mix the pecans, raisins, and cinnamon. Stuff each apple with ¼ of the mixture.

Put the apples into a 9-inch round microwave baking dish. Cover with plastic wrap. Microwave on high for 4 to 5 minutes, rotating the dish once. Let stand for 5 minutes. Serves 4.

HOCUS-POCUS HALAVAH

1 cup tahini (sesame seed paste)

6 cups confectioners' sugar

In a food processor, blend the tahini until smooth. Add 2 to 2½ cups of the confectioners' sugar. Process to combine for about 30 seconds. The mixture should be a thick paste. Add more sugar (or a few drops of vegetable oil) to achieve the proper consistency. Place the remaining sugar in a small pan. Roll rounded teaspoons of the tahini mixture into ½-inch balls. Roll the balls in the confectioners' sugar to coat. Chill for about 3 hours. Remove from sugar to serve. Yields 25 pieces.

ERETZ ESROG CAKE

Vegetable oil spray
1 esrog
1 lime, juice only
1 tbsp. lemon juice
2¾ cups cake flour
3 tsp. baking powder
¼ tsp. salt

¾ cup margarine
1½ cups sugar
3 eggs
1 cup plus 1 tbsp. orange juice
1 cup confectioners' sugar
1 tsp. vanilla

Preheat the oven to 375 degrees. Spray a tube pan with vegetable oil spray. Grate the esrog peel and add the lime juice, lemon juice, and juice from the esrog. (Strain the esrog juice through cheesecloth because it is very membranous and has dozens of seeds.) Reserve 1 tablespoon of the citrus mixture for the glaze.

Sift the flour, baking powder, and salt together. Cream the margarine with the sugar until fluffy. Add the citrus mixture and blend. Add the eggs and beat well. Alternate adding half of the flour mixture with the cup of orange juice, beating well after each addition. Pour into the prepared tube pan and bake in a 375-degree oven for 45 minutes, or until cake tests done.

Blend together reserved tablespoon of citrus mixture, confectioners sugar, the tablespoon of orange juice, and vanilla. Remove the cake from the pan and, while cake is still warm, drizzle glaze on top. Serves 10.

MAZELDICK MANDELBROT

1 cup margarine
1½ cups sugar
4 eggs
1 tsp. vanilla

4 cups flour
4 tsp. baking powder
1 tsp. salt
1 cup slivered almonds

Beat the margarine and sugar together until light and fluffy. Blend in the eggs and vanilla. Combine the dry ingredients and add them to the mixture. Mix well. Stir in the almonds. Spread the batter evenly into a greased-and-floured, 15x10x1-inch jelly roll pan. Bake at 350 degrees for 30 to 35 minutes, or until golden brown. Cut into 3 ⅓ by ¾-inch slices. Place each slice, cut side up, on a cookie sheet; then broil for 1 to 2 minutes on each side or until lightly browned. Makes approximately 4 dozen pieces.

RUCHEL'S RUGELACH

1½ cups unsifted flour
2 tbsp. sugar
1 tsp. salt
2 3-oz. pkg. cream cheese
½ cup peanut oil

¼ cup sugar
½ tsp. cinnamon
1 egg white, stiffly beaten
½ cup finely chopped pecans
   or walnuts

Combine the flour, 2 tablespoons of sugar, and salt. Cut in the cheese with a pastry blender until the mixture resembles a coarse meal. Add the peanut oil and blend with a fork.

On a lightly floured board, roll the dough to ⅛-inch thickness. Cut with a 3-inch cookie cutter. Place on ungreased baking sheets. Mix the rest of the sugar and cinnamon; then gently fold it into the beaten egg white. Fold in the chopped nuts. Place 1 rounded teaspoon of filling in the center of each dough circle. Fold and seal the edges. Sprinkle with additional sugar-cinnamon mix, if desired. Bake in a 400-degree oven for 15 minutes, or until lightly browned around the edges. Makes about 2½ dozen miniature pastries.

SHALOM AND KOL-TOV
"Peace" and "All-Good"

In an extended effort to expand the horizon of Kosher cuisine, we have traveled the eleven southern states known as the Confederacy. We studied their origins, settling, growth, traditions, and foods; and we found a striking parallel with the Jewish people and their history.

We have tried to demonstrate to our readers the continuity of a people through their trials and tribulations. We have faced wars together and, in the end, we have been able to achieve a way of life filled with festive celebration that focuses on food and always includes family and friends.

There was even a musical commonality. The songs of Dixie, the songs of a united America, and the songs of the Jewish homeland of Israel seem to express the same thoughts—love of land and pride in their people. Yes, we have all emerged as one.

We leave you now with a closing song and the traditional Jewish Hebrew greeting: *Shalom Aleichem* and *Aleichem Sholem,* "Peace Unto You" and "Unto You Peace."

GLOSSARY

Adobe: sun dried bricks used in Mexico and elsewhere for building houses.

Al dente: literally translates to "to the tooth." Refers to pastas and sometimes vegetables cooked until tender but still slightly firm.

Alef baze: the Hebrew alphabet; Hebrew ABC's.

Aleichem Sholem: greeting meaning "unto you peace."

Alibamu: tribe of Indians of the Creek Confederacy; translates to "thicket clearers" or "plant gatherers."

Antebellum: period before the Civil War

Balabatish: quiet, respectable; of some consequence.

Baste: to spoon cooking juices, fat, or a marinade over food as it cooks to help keep it moist.

Beef Frye: Kosher sliced cured smoked plate beef.

Behayma: an animal, especially a cow.

Bonditt: son-of-a-gun.

Borscht: beet soup.

Braise: brown foods lightly first in a little fat, then moistened with liquid and cooked slowly, usually tightly covered.

Broite: Yiddish for bread.

Cajun: descendant of French colonists exiled from Nova Scotia who settled in southern Louisiana.

Canape: a toasted piece of bread or cracker topped with variety of spreads and served as an appetizer.

Carpetbagger: a northern officeholder in the South during the period of Reconstruction after the Civil War who took advantage of the unsettled conditions; contemptuous term, referring to the fact that such men usually carried all their belongings in a single carpetbag.

Chai: Hebrew for "life"; also Hebrew for the number 18.

Chelm: fictional city in Jewish folklore.

Chitterlings: called "chittlins;" the small intestines of an animal, used for food.

Chowder: an American dish usually consisting of fried onions, pieces of fish or seasoned meat, potatoes, and seasoned with spices and simmered in a saucepan.

Chutzpa: gall, nerve.

Cilantro: the green coriander leaf frequently added to Mexican dishes.

Confederacy: the group of southern states that seceded from the United States in 1860 and 1861; also called Confederate States of America; Southern Confederacy.

Conquistador: any one of the Spanish conquerors of South or Central America in the 16th century.

Crab Boil: commercial name for a combination of various spices, tied in a bag and used for seasoning seafoods.

Cracker: an impoverished white person in the rural sections of the southern United States, especially in Georgia.

Creole: descendant of original French and Spanish settlers of Louisiana.

Cuzinee: cousin.

Dauphin: a name assumed around the middle of the 9th century by the lord of the French province of Dauphiny; a title used by the eldest son of the King of France from 1349 to 1830.

Delta: a triangular-shaped tract of alluvial land at the mouth of the Mississippi River.

Dixie: popular name for the ten-dollar bank note issued in Louisiana prior to the Civil War, so called from the large "dix" (meaning ten) printed on one side; also the Southern States of the United States, collectively; a song celebrating the South, composed in 1859 by D. D. Emmett (it became popular in the Confederacy during the Civil War).

Emmes: Yiddish for truth or truly.

Eretz: land, as in Eretz Yisroel (Promised Land of Israel).

Esrog: one of 4 species of plants used in Succoth ceremony; resembles large lemon, but not botanically related.

Farpotshket: Jewish potpourri.

Filé: powder made from dried sassafras leaves, used as thickening agent.

Florida: from Spanish word meaning flowers.

Frappéd: partly frozen; iced.

Fraylich: carefree, gay, happy.

Fresser: a glutton.

Fricasse: dish made of poultry or meat stewed slowly in gravy.

Fritters: small amount of batter containing fruit, fish, vegetables, or other ingredients, fried in deep oil or sautéed.

Frummeh: pious.

Gahntze tzimmes: a whole production.

Galitzianer: A Jew from Galicia, a province of Poland/Austria.

Gateau: a rich cake made usually with a butter sponge or Genoese sponge foundation and decorated with icing, cream, jam, nuts, or butter cream.

Gefilte fish: a combination of various fish, chopped, or ground, mixed with onion, egg, seasoning, etc.; cooked and usually served as an appetizer.

Genoese: a rich sponge cake mixture or a sauce.

Genug: enough!

Gottenyu: good heavens; Oh, dear Lord!

Grits: coarsely ground hominy; indigenous to the South.

Gullah: a Creole language spoken by Afro-Americans, descendants of slaves, who live in the Low Country of South Carolina and Georgia.

Gumbo: highly seasoned thick soup made with okra and filé.

Hacienda: Spanish American large estate, ranch, or house in the country.

Haimish: cozy, warm; happy home.

Hase: hot.

Hatikvah: national anthem of the State of Israel; literally means "the hope."

Haute cuisine: the preparation of fine food by highly skilled chefs; or the food so prepared.

Hava Nagila: Hebrew folk song; literally translated "come let us rejoice."

Hora: an Israeli folk dance.

Huguenot: any French Protestant of the 16th or 17th century.

Hush puppies: rounds of fried cornmeal

Indigo: plant of the pea family that yields a blue dye.
Isinglass: a form of gelatin prepared from the internal membranes of fish bladder; used as clarifying agent and adhesive.

Jambalaya: a rice dish containing seafood, meat, or poultry.
Jigger: liquid measurement equal to 1½ ounces.

Kalleh: bride.
Kasha: cracked buckwheat or wheat cooked into a mushlike consistency and served with meat or in soup.
Kibbitzer: one who teases and humors one along.
Kibbutz: cooperative settlement in Israel; a collective group.
Klezmer: itinerant Eastern European musician.
Kol-tov: greeting wishing one "all-good."
Kosher: foods adhering to Jewish dietary laws.
Kugel: a pudding usually made of noodles sometimes with fruit and cheeses; also made with potatoes or rice.

Leffel: spoon.
Luntsmon: someone who comes from the same town; in Europe, a fellow countryman.

Macher: someone who arranges or fixes; an operator.
Maven: a Jewish "know-it-all."
Mazeldick: lucky.
Metsieh: a lucky break.
Mince: to chop very fine.
Minorcans: natives of Minorca, a Spanish island located in the Western Mediterranean near Majorca.
Mish-mosh: a hodge-podge.
Mishpocheh: the extended family.
Mississippi: Indian word meaning "great river" or "great waters;" river also called the Father of Waters.
Mousse: a light airy dish usually containing either beaten egg whites, cream, or gelatin.

Nachas: special joy, pride, pleasure.
Noyeau: (also spelled noyau) fruit stones, the kernels of which, with spirit, provide strongly flavored liqueurs used to flavor puddings, creams, and punches.

Paella: dish of rice with meat or chicken.
Palmetto: any of several species of palm trees growing in the West Indies and southern part of the United States.
Parboil: to partially cook food by boiling as a preliminary step.
Pareve: foods that may be served with either dairy or meat dishes.
Plantation: an estate, as in a tropical or semitropical region cultivated by the workers living on it.
Pone: in the southern part of the United States, bread, loaf or cake made of cornmeal.
Potpourri: a miscellaneous collection.
Poulet: French term for chicken.
Puree: to mash ingredients until completely smooth.

Quartern: a fourth part, a quarter; one-fourth of a pint, a gill; one-fourth of a peck.

Ratafias: a liqueur or cordial flavored with the kernels of almonds or fruit, particularly of cherries or apricots; name of a sweet, small, almond-flavored biscuit.
Rebel: name applied to those who fought on the side of the South in the Civil War.
Reconstruction: the process after the Civil War or reorganizing the southern states that had seceded and re-establishing them in the Union; the period between 1867-1877.
Reduce: to concentrate liquids by boiling them uncovered. As the water evaporates, the liquid becomes thicker and more intense in flavor.
Render: to melt animal fat such as chicken, duck, beef, by slow cooking.
Roita: the color red.
Roux: basic mixture of flour and shortening used to thicken sauces, gravies, and soups.

Rozhinkes: raisins.

Sack: any of various strong, light-colored dry wines from Spain and the Canary Islands, popular in England in the 16th and 17th centuries.

Sauté: to fry lightly in very little fat.

Scalawag: a tricky or worthless person; term used to refer to a white Southerner who was a Republican during the Reconstruction following the Civil War; an opprobrious term used by southern Democrats.

Scald: to heat a liquid until it nearly, but not quite, boils.

Schlepper: figuratively—a drag, a jerk, a nerd.

Schmaltz: rendered chicken fat.

Score: to cut shallow incisions into food.

Seminole: a member of a tribe of American Indians who settled in Florida; the word translates to mean "wild."

Shah! shah!: an order to be quiet.

Shallots: a breed of the onion whose bulb is used for flavoring; interchangeable with green onions or scallions.

Shalom: a greeting wishing one "peace."

Shalom Aleichem: greeting meaning "peace unto you."

Shavuot: Jewish holiday commemorating the handing down of the Ten Commandments to the Children of Israel; the agricultural festival marking end of Spring harvest.

Shissel: a plate or pan.

Shtetl: small village in Jewish communities of Eastern Europe.

Sieva bean: a variety of the lima bean family.

Simcha: joyous occasion; happy celebration.

Simchat torah: holiday following 8 days of Succoth that celebrates the conclusion of the annual cycle of reading the Torah. Literally, "the day of rejoicing in the law."

Simmer: to cook gently in hot liquid just below a boil.

Sourmash: whiskey made by using a mash that has already been fermented to make ordinary whiskey.

Succah: temporary booths built during the Children of Israel's journey in the desert; re-created during the holiday of Succoth.

Succoth: 8-day holiday celebrating the fall harvest and God's protectiveness of the children of Israel in the desert.

Suet: the fatty tissue of cattle and sheep, particularly the hard, crumbly fat deposited around the kidneys and loins; used in cooking and making tallow.

Syllabub: a dessert or beverage made by blending wine or cider with cream or milk, producing a light, frothy appearance.

Taka: true, real.

Tante: Yiddish for Aunt.

Tart, tarte: a small pastry shell, containing fruit, jam, or jelly without a top crust.

Tata: affectionate term for father.

Tomatillos: a sour variety of green tomato used in Mexican sauces.

Torah: scroll containing the Five Books of Moses.

Torte: a cake made with many eggs and often with grated nuts or dry bread crumbs covered with a rich frosting; a rich gateau with fruit, cream, etc.

Tunkler: dusk, twilight time.

Vulcan: in Roman mythology, the god who presided over fire and the working of metals.

Wiener schnitzel: a popular German and Viennese dish of veal cutlets usually sliced thin, coated with eggs and crumbs, then fried.

Yams: southern sweet potatoes.

Yellowhammer: gaily colored bird, a small European finch; also known as flicker in North America.

Zayde: grandfather.

Zeese: sweet.

Zest: the thin, colored, oily outer skin of citrus fruits, particularly orange and lemon, which is frequently used for flavoring and coloring.

MICROWAVE INDEX

INDEX